P9-AQL-982

SWEET HOME CAFE

COOKBOOK

A CELEBRATION OF AFRICAN AMERICAN COOKING

✠

Albert G. Lukas and **Jessica B. Harris,** with
contributions by **Jerome Grant**

Foreword by **Lonnie G. Bunch III**

Introduction by **Jacquelyn D. Serwer**

In Association with the
**National Museum of African American
History and Culture** and
Restaurant Associates

Smithsonian Books
WASHINGTON, DC

This book may be purchased for educational, business, or sales promotional use.

For information, please write: Special Markets Department, Smithsonian Books, P.O. Box 37012, MRC 513, Washington, DC 20013.

Headnotes and sidebars by Jessica B. Harris. Café menu development and recipes by Supervising Chef Albert G. Lukas (unless otherwise noted). Culinary Cousins recipes by Executive Chef Jerome Grant. Designed by Gary Tooth / Empire Design Studio. Food photography by Scott Suchman, with propping by Kristi Hunter. Food styling by Lisa Cherkasky, with assistance from Carolyn Robb. Objects and historical photographs from collections of the National Museum of African American History and Culture. Edited by Sharon Silva. Recipes edited by Merideth Tennant and Susan Stuck.

National Museum of African American History and Culture Director: Lonnie G. Bunch III. Cookbook Development Team: Kinshasha Holman Conwill, Jacquelyn D. Serwer, John Franklin. Content Specialist Advisors: Elaine Nichols, Joanne Hyppolite. Photo Research: Douglas Remley.

Restaurant Associates George Conomos, Vice President. Albert G. Lukas, Supervising Chef. Jerome Grant, Executive Chef.

Published by Smithsonian Books Director: Carolyn Gleason. Creative Director: Jody Billert. Senior Editor: Christina Wiginton. Editorial Assistant: Jaime Schwender. Editorial Consultant: Duke Johns.

Library of Congress Cataloging-in-Publication Data

Names: Lukas, Albert, 1968– author. | Harris, Jessica B., author.

Title: Sweet Home Café cookbook : a celebration of African American cooking /

Albert Lukas and Jessica B. Harris, with contributions by Jerome Grant ;

foreword by Lonnie G. Bunch III ; introduction by Jacquelyn Serwer.

Description: Washington, DC : Smithsonian Books, 2018. | Includes

bibliographical references and index.

Identifiers: LCCN 2018016725 | ISBN 9781588346407 (hardcover)

Subjects: LCSH: African American cooking. | Cooking, American—Southern

style. | Sweet Home Café. | LCGFT: Cookbooks.

Classification: LCC TX715.2.A47 L85 2018 | DDC 641.59/296073—dc23 LC record available at https://lccn.loc.gov/2018016725

Manufactured in China, not at government expense

22 21 20 19 18   5 4 3 2 1

Food photography by Scott Suchman, unless otherwise noted.

National Museum of African American History and Culture: Frontispiece: TA2014.306.5.3.1, Gift of the Scurlock family; 10: 2012.56.1.16, © Douglas Keister; 12: 2012.107.16, © Danny Lyon/Magnum Photos; 13: 2015.97.42; 16, top left: 2014.82.2, Gift of Dr. Deborah L. Mack, © 2008 Southern Food & Beverage Museum; 16, top right: 2015.37.3; 16, bottom right: 2017.49.14, Gift of Pete Marovich, © Pete Marovich; 18, top right: 2009.36.4, Gift of Brigitte Freed in memory of Leonard Freed, © Leonard Freed/Magnum; 18, bottom left: 2015.50.1ab; 47, top: 2014.312.172, Gift of Oprah Winfrey; 47, bottom: 2011.155.172; 54, bottom: 2014.310.37, Generously donated by Bank of America Corporation, © Jeanne Moutoussamy-Ashe; 55, top: 2016.27.11, Gift of the Heilig Family Descendants; 55, bottom: 2014.150.5.25, © Estate of Lloyd W. Yearwood; 56: 2014.63.63.37; 57, top: 2014.37.36.6; 57, bottom: 2014.63.63.2ab; 70, top: 2011.15.262, Gift of Milton Williams Archives, © Milton Williams; 70, bottom: 2015.36.2; 74, top left: 2013.197.7, © Dawoud Bey; 74, bottom right: 2014.268ab, © Gustave Blache III; 75, top: 2011.15.217, Gift of Milton Williams Archives, © Milton Williams; 74, bottom: 2017.14.4, Gift of the Stokes/Washington Family; 76: 2014.210.2, Gift of Jessica B. Harris; 77: 2007.1.69.13.29.B, © Smithsonian National Museum of African American History and Culture; 84, top: 2017.49.16, Gift of Pete Marovich, © Pete Marovich; 84, bottom: 2013.225.1-.3, Gift of Deborah T. Salahu-Din; 107, top: 2012.149.5, © Pirkle Jones Foundation; 107, bottom: 2015.97.26.25; 126, top left: TA2015.143.3.17, Gift of Jennifer Cain Bohrnstedt; 126, top middle: 2009.50.35ab, Gift of Charles L. Blockson; 126, bottom middle: 2011.165.25, Gift of Howard and Ellen Greenberg; 127, bottom right: 2010.14; 129: 2015.97.26.28; 132: 2011.165.45, Gift of Howard and Ellen Greenberg, © The Aaron Siskind Foundation; 160, top left: 2014.276.2.16, Gift of Graham Holdings Company, © Robert H. McNeill; 160, top middle: 2017.26.2, © The Aaron Siskind Foundation; 161, bottom right: 2013.46.25.222; 163, top: 2013.39.7, Gift of the family of Becca Nu'Mani; 163, middle: 2010.74.57, Gift of Joe Schwartz and Family, © Joe Schwartz; 163, bottom: 2012.141.41, © Jason Miccolo Johnson; 194, top left: 2011.165.14, Gift of Howard and Ellen Greenberg; 194, bottom middle: 2014.150.5.32, © Estate of Lloyd W. Yearwood; 195: 2015.97.26.26.

Front cover (clockwise from bottom right): A feast featuring Baked Macaroni & Cheese (p. 45), Yellow Corn Bread (p. 151), Buttermilk Fried Chicken (p. 103), Texas Caviar (p. 144), Tomato-Watermelon Salad (p. 20), and Dilly Green Beans (p. 133).

Page 1: The Scurlock family celebrating a birthday, 1915. Page 2: Frogmore Stew (p. 59). Page 4: Baked Macaroni & Cheese (p. 45).

CONTENTS

❃

**ABOUT THE
SWEET HOME CAFÉ**
8

INTRODUCTION
10

SALADS AND SIDES
14

SOUPS AND STEWS
52

MAINS
72

**PICKLES, SNACKS,
AND BREADS**
124

SWEETS AND DRINKS
158

BASICS
192

RECIPE LIST BY REGION
204

MENUS
207

ACKNOWLEDGMENTS
208

BIBLIOGRAPHY
210

INDEX
211

The Sweet Home
Café offers a respite
for visitors and also
serves as an extension
of the museum's
exhibitions. Graphic
panels on the café
walls explore the ways
that African American
cooking and food
culture have shaped
American food.

ABOUT THE
SWEET HOME CAFÉ

❋

BY LONNIE G. BUNCH III

FOUNDING DIRECTOR, SMITHSONIAN NATIONAL MUSEUM OF
AFRICAN AMERICAN HISTORY AND CULTURE

I OFTEN THINK BACK to September 24, 2016, the day the National Museum of African American History and Culture was dedicated and opened for the American people. As I sat nervously on the stage with President and Mrs. Obama, President and Mrs. Bush, Chief Justice Roberts, Congressman John Lewis, and a dizzying array of dignitaries and celebrities, I remembered how we had worked to create a museum that would use the African American experience as the lens through which to understand what it means to be Americans. To achieve that goal, the museum had to serve and embrace everyone regardless of race. That is why I ended my remarks by saying, "Welcome home." But what is a home without a space of welcome, a place to gather, a site to come together to debate, reflect, smile, and chat over good food? The Sweet Home Café, with its award-winning regional cuisine, warmly and wonderfully fulfills that dream.

Whenever I walk through the Sweet Home Café, I am so moved to see our visitors seated over a shared meal, discussing their experiences in the museum with people previously unknown to them; reflecting upon how this history and culture has shaped or enlightened them; and grappling with the questions and uncertainties that inform our world today. We designed the café to be a space for families and for conversation, where fine food allows visitors to come together, despite our contentious history, to find a shared past and to work for a common future.

Many of the recipes in this cookbook have been passed down through the generations, reflecting both the power of family and the centrality of food. My own life is ripe with memories of family discussions around the kitchen table, tasting one of my mother's many recipe-driven meals. While some were forgettable (sorry, Mom), others—like her banana pudding rimmed with vanilla wafers—still stay with me nearly a half century later. These recipes tell us much about a people, about a culture. With every wonderful bite, we remember and we honor all of our ancestors.

I am honored to dedicate this cookbook to my mother, Montrose Boone Bunch, and to all those women who labored, who cooked, and whose efforts maintained our families.

9

Picnickers enjoy a sunny afternoon in a Lincoln, Nebraska, backyard.
Photographer John Johnson recorded the vibrant African American
community in Lincoln from 1910 to 1925.

INTRODUCTION

BY JACQUELYN D. SERWER

CHIEF CURATOR, SMITHSONIAN NATIONAL MUSEUM OF
AFRICAN AMERICAN HISTORY AND CULTURE

FOOD, FAMILY, FRIENDS—they all go together. Our most memorable gatherings, from casual family dinners to formal holiday feasts, revolve around the restorative experience of a shared meal. Most of us seek out occasions whose centerpiece is good food, and many of us love to prepare food as much as—or even more than—we like to eat it.

The *Sweet Home Café Cookbook*, named for the restaurant at the National Museum of African American History and Culture and featuring many of the dishes served there, offers a rewarding and comforting collection of recipes that will satisfy both cooks and diners. It draws on our nation's long culinary history and on the many significant contributions made to it by African Americans, both in public establishments as chefs and restaurateurs and in private homes as cooks and housekeepers, and it showcases the prominence of African American foodways in our national cuisine. In recent years, dishes that were once considered to be strictly black southern food—greens, grits, and shrimp gumbo are among the best-known examples—have become classics of American cuisine and are highlighted on menus across the country, and celebrated African American chefs and cooks, including Leah Chase, Edna Lewis, Barbara "B." Smith, Patrick Clark, and Vertamae Smart-Grosvenor, are now recognized as having reshaped the national table as a whole.

The book reflects both the diasporic legacy of African Americans and the wide geographic reach of their foodways. Black cooking in America includes not only the culinary traditions of Africa and the Caribbean but also the influences of Native Americans, Europeans, Latinos, and contemporary immigrants from African countries and other nations around the world. All of these mingled elements have combined into a culinary heritage that is broad, deep, and continually evolving in surprising new ways.

This collection reminds readers of the cleverness of black home cooks, who, with limited funds and often little access to a broad spectrum of ingredients, could nonetheless produce culinary masterpieces. That resourcefulness also calls to mind the contributions of enslaved black chefs such as Old Doll and Hercules, both of whom cooked for George Washington. Hercules accompanied President Washington to Philadelphia—at that time the temporary capital of the United States—and later managed to escape and free himself.

Student Nonviolent Coordinating Committee (SNCC) staff and supporters, including Taylor Washington, Ivanhoe Donaldson, Joyce Ladner, John Lewis, Judy Richardson, George Greene, and Seku Neblett, take a break from a conference to join a sit-in at a Toddle House restaurant.

Atlanta, Georgia. A Toddle House during a Sit-In, 1963; printed 1994. Photograph by Danny Lyon.

The legendary black eating establishments—both past and present—in urban centers around the country have also inspired the recipes in this book. Among them are Thomas Downing's Oyster House, a celebrated nineteenth-century restaurant in New York City that, ironically, served only white patrons; Patillo's Bar-B-Q in Beaumont, Texas, in operation since 1912; Sylvia's Restaurant in Harlem, a popular eatery that opened in 1962; Jones Bar-B-Q Diner in Marianna, Arkansas, recognized as one of the oldest continuously operated black-owned restaurants in the South; and the Florida Avenue Grill in Washington, DC, which opened in 1944 and continues to flourish in its original Northwest DC neighborhood.

The constraints and challenges that African American cooks have faced throughout history—ranging from a lack of necessary ingredients for some to a lack of the basic freedom to break bread with family and friends for others—did not prevent them from crafting rich cooking traditions under a variety of circumstances. Urban black people adapted to the offerings of small neighborhood markets, bodegas, and grocery stores. Rural people, meanwhile, who often depended on the fruits, vegetables, and meats they could raise on the land, put together nutritious and flavorful dishes that took advantage of homegrown ingredients. Traditions varied across the country, and thus the recipes of both the Sweet Home Café and this book focus on four main geographic areas: the Agricultural South, the Creole Coast, the Northern States, and the Western Range.

Cooks and readers who want to learn more about the culinary customs that inspired the recipes in the Café and this book will find much to explore in the galleries of the National Museum of African American History and Culture itself. Exhibitions on the museum's second floor, for example, focus on the *Green Book*, that indispensable handbook to eating establishments and lodging that guided

African Americans traveling the American South during the era of segregation. They offer a reminder of the perils and challenges faced by black families whenever they journeyed away from home in the pre–civil rights era.

In the Segregation section of the museum's history galleries, visitors will find the Greensboro Lunch Counter interactive, where a touch table offers information on this important episode in the civil rights struggle; keep exploring the gallery and you will see a stool from the lunch counter on display. Another evocation of the Greensboro protest can be found in the Sweet Home Café, where a large photo mural of the young civil rights activists greets visitors as they enter.

On the fourth floor, the Cultural Expressions exhibition highlights food traditions. Cherished pots, pans, and platters reflect the passing down of cooking tools through the generations, and the varied cookbooks on display document African American contributions to sharing and archiving their culinary inventions. Some of the images and artifacts from the civil rights era bring to mind the many southern families who, despite their modest circumstances, provided hearty meals for civil rights workers and student activists, and sometimes boarded them when they had no other safe place to stay.

Although this cookbook certainly connects to stories in the museum, it also offers a treasure trove of recipes that will appeal to every food lover, whether he or she is familiar with this foundational American cuisine or is new to trad-itional African American cooking. Compiled with the guidance of Sweet Home Café chefs Albert Lukas and Jerome Grant of Restaurant Associates and noted culinary historian Jessica B. Harris, who helped shape the Café concept, these recipes provide a wealth of ideas for both everyday family meals and special occasions. Favoring fresh, seasonal ingredients, the recipes translate the dishes of black family lore for the contemporary palate, adding easy-to-follow instructions for novice cooks and emphasiz-ing preparations that rely on less sugar, salt, and fat. You'll discover innovative ways to appreciate familiar ingredients and encounter intriguing new ones, such as cuts of meat overlooked by haute cuisine. You'll even find recipes that reflect current shifts in African American cooking, like vegan dishes and reduced prep time, as well as special menus for holiday get-togethers, such as Christmas, New

Year's, and Juneteenth. Helpful tips on preparation and presentation round out the book's offerings.

Most of all, the *Sweet Home Café Cookbook* is intended to recall and celebrate a family's happiest memories, because heritage and nostalgia play central roles in African American cooking. These recipes highlight the joys of good, hearty food and the pleasures of continuing traditions that have always been at the foundation of African American family life. You'll find the book entertaining even if you only read the recipes, but you'll discover it is most satisfying when you prepare the dishes and enjoy the results. With these recipes in hand, you can create memorable meals for everyone who sits at your table.

Savor this book, bask in the appreciation of your family and friends, and relish the rewards of making delicious food for the people you love.

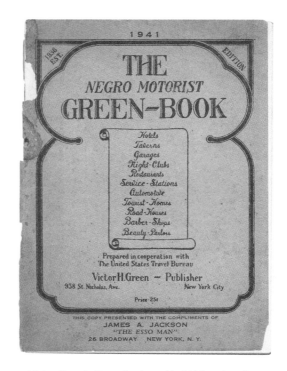

Victor Green's *Green Book* provided African Americans traveling in the United States during the era of segregation with lists of friendly eating establishments and lodging.

SALADS
AND
SIDES

PICKLED GULF SHRIMP

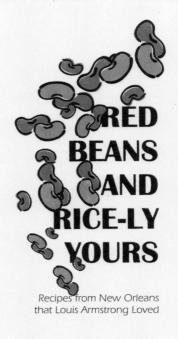

RED BEANS AND RICE-LY YOURS

Recipes from New Orleans that Louis Armstrong Loved

By Christopher Blake

Pineapples and Bananas.

STEWED TOMATOES & OKRA

Opposite, top left: A collection of traditional New Orleans recipes, many of which were served at a dinner accompanying one of Louis Armstrong's final public performances on January 29, 1971.

Opposite, top right: Postcard of a pineapple and banana vendor in Florida, 1912.

Opposite, bottom right: *Gullah man farming lettuce, St. Helena Island, SC*, 2004-14. Photograph by Pete Marovich.

SALADS
AND
SIDES

Feature: Creole Coast / 18

Tomato-Watermelon Salad / 20

Sweet Pea Tendril Salad / 22

Field Green Salad / 23

Baby Kale Salad / 25

Potato Salad / 26

Coleslaw / 27

Pickled Gulf Shrimp / 29

Stewed Tomatoes & Okra / 30

Feature: Okra / 32

Kale Sprouts with Sorghum
& Benne / 33

Slow-Cooked Collards & Potlikker / 34

Stewed Black-Eyed Peas / 35

Mixed Greens with Baby Turnips / 37

Fried Green Tomatoes / 38

Corn Pudding / 39

Fried Okra / 41

Ginger & Brown Sugar
Candied Sweet Potatoes / 42

Yankee Baked Beans / 43

Baked Macaroni & Cheese / 45

Hoppin' John / 46

Feature: Rice / 47

Carolina Gold Rice Pilaf / 48

Rice & Pigeon Peas / 49

Louis Armstrong's Red Beans & Rice / 51

CREOLE COAST

In this coastal area, which runs from Charleston to New Orleans and includes parts of South Carolina, Georgia, Florida, Alabama, Mississippi, and Louisiana, local foodways traditionally mixed and mingled with those of Europe, Africa, and the Caribbean as well as with those of Native Americans through extended contacts within the Atlantic world. In the more remote areas of the region, such as the Sea Islands that run from Georgia to north Florida, food was defined by people who retained close culinary ties to their African motherlands.

The Creole Coast is a rice-eating world, where a love of rice and a deep knowledge of its cultivation have led to a unique style of cooking that celebrates the grain in pilafs (called purloos in South Carolina) such as Hoppin' John, red rice, and Louisiana's jambalaya. In South Carolina the task system used in cultivating rice, in which each slave was assigned a daily job to finish and then was free to do as he or she wished, meant that some of the enslaved had time to grow their own foods. Occasionally they sold them in the region's towns, and their street cries created a distinctive soundscape that was acknowledged by writers and musicians alike.

In twentieth-century New Orleans, Lena Richard, in one of the region's many firsts, went from caterer and cooking school instructor to cookbook author to television star in 1949, becoming the first African American to host a cooking show on television.

Two decades later, author and culinary anthropologist Vertamae Smart-Grosvenor penned *Vibration Cooking, or the Travel Notes of a Geechee Girl*, and single-handedly rehabilitated the word *Geechee*, revalorizing it in the context of the culture's links to Africa.

The diversity of the people of the Creole Coast is reflected especially in the region's rich gumbos, which range from the roux-free versions of Charleston to the mahogany roux–thickened Cajun stews of Louisiana. Gumbo recipes even vary from household to household, with no absolute guidelines other than those of the family grandmother. These lively kitchens of coastal living also make abundant use of both local seafood and the culinary traditions of France, Spain, and the rice-growing areas of West Africa, all of which contribute to this region's place among the country's most storied cuisines.

SHRIMP & GRITS

Opposite, top right: *A full-service vendor in Dryades Street. New Orleans • USA*, 1965. Photograph by Leonard Freed.

Opposite, bottom left: A traditional sweet-grass basket used to store rice; made by Mary A. Jackson. Charleston, South Carolina, 2014.

DUCK & CRAWFISH GUMBO

SERVES
6 to 8

ACTIVE TIME
20 MINS
🕐
TOTAL TIME
20 MINS

VEGETARIAN

TOMATO-WATERMELON
SALAD

THIS SALAD COMBINES TWO favorites of the summer garden. For an especially attractive plate, use a selection of height-of-the-season heirloom tomatoes in various colors with juicy red and/or yellow watermelon.

CHEF'S NOTE

This is a great summer salad that combines crisp, sweet, juicy watermelon with the season's most flavorful tomatoes. If yellow watermelons such as 'Moon and Stars' or 'Yellow Buttercup' are available, try mixing them with red melons.

6 mixed vine-ripened heirloom tomatoes (such as Brandywine, Cherokee Purple, or German Green)

2½ pounds seedless watermelon

½ cup extra-virgin olive oil

3 tablespoons sherry vinegar

1 teaspoon fine sea salt

Freshly ground black pepper

1 pinch Espelette pepper or cayenne pepper

½ cup Vidalia or other sweet onion, thinly sliced

¼ cup fresh flat-leaf parsley, coarsely chopped

Core the tomatoes and cut into wedges.

Cut the green skin off the watermelon, trimming away the white rind and exposing the flesh. Cut the flesh into large dice.

In a large salad bowl, whisk the olive oil, vinegar, salt, black pepper to taste, and the Espelette pepper until a light emulsion forms. Add the watermelon, tomatoes, and onion and toss well. Add the parsley, taste and adjust the seasoning with salt and pepper, and toss again before serving.

SERVES

4 to 6

ACTIVE TIME
25 MINS
🕐
TOTAL TIME
25 MINS

VEGETARIAN

SWEET PEA
TENDRIL SALAD

UNTIL RECENTLY, PEA TENDRILS (also called pea shoots), the small, young leaves, stems, and vines of the snow pea plant, were difficult to find. Now they are more widely available, putting this delightfully toothsome salad more easily within reach. Dress the salad lightly to enjoy more fully its crisp yet delicate texture and subtle pea flavor.

CHEF'S NOTE

This salad is light on the dressing and heavy on the crunch. Crisp, lightly dressed vegetables make it a versatile complement for many entrées.

1 teaspoon sherry vinegar

¼ teaspoon Dijon mustard

1 pinch sea salt

Freshly ground black pepper

2 tablespoons extra-virgin olive oil

1 pound sweet pea tendrils, washed and dried, thick stems discarded

2 carrots, peeled and shaved into thin ribbons with a mandoline or horizontal vegetable peeler

6 radishes (such as French breakfast or icicle), thinly sliced

½ Vidalia or other sweet onion, thinly sliced

In a small bowl, combine the vinegar, mustard, salt, and pepper to taste. Slowly whisk in the olive oil until a light emulsion has formed.

In a large serving bowl, combine the tendrils, carrots, radishes, and onion. Drizzle in just enough of the vinaigrette to lightly coat the vegetables and tendrils, and serve.

FIELD GREEN SALAD

CONTINENTAL
UNITED STATES

SERVES
4 to **6**

ACTIVE TIME
15 MINS

TOTAL TIME
15 MINS

VEGETARIAN

A MIX OF SALAD GREENS— young lettuces, other baby greens, and herbs—is called *mesclun* in the Provençal dialect of southern France. Look for a blend made up of the smallest, most tender leaves whether shopping at a farmer's market or a supermarket. When adding the vinaigrette, use a light, even hand; every leaf should just glisten.

CHEF'S NOTE

If you cannot locate spiced pecans, make the Sea Salt–Spiced Cocktail Nuts on page 140 using only pecans. The Café uses heirloom tomatoes, but if they are unavailable you can substitute grape, teardrop, or plum tomatoes.

¼ teaspoon Dijon mustard

⅛ teaspoon kosher salt

1 teaspoon minced shallot

⅛ cup cider vinegar

½ cup pecan oil, almond, peanut oil, or extra-virgin olive oil

1 pound local seasonal field greens, washed and dried

1 cup baby heirloom tomatoes, halved

1 large European cucumber, peeled and thinly sliced

1 carrot, peeled and shaved into thin ribbons with a mandoline or horizontal vegetable peeler

Freshly ground black pepper

¾ cup spiced pecans

In a small bowl, combine the mustard, salt, shallot, and vinegar. Slowly whisk in the oil until a light emulsion has formed.

In a large bowl, toss the greens with the tomatoes, cucumber, and carrot. Drizzle the dressing over the greens and gently toss to fully coat the salad. Season with pepper to taste. Transfer to a serving bowl, top with the pecans, and serve immediately.

BABY KALE
SALAD

CONTINENTAL
UNITED STATES

SERVES
4 to **6**

ACTIVE TIME
20 MINS

TOTAL TIME
30 MINS

IN AFRICAN AMERICAN HOUSE-holds, kale has traditionally been cooked long and low, with a piece of seasoning meat. Today, it is just as likely to turn up in a great-tasting salad like this one.

CHEF'S NOTE

Buy the freshest kale you can find, then rinse the leaves carefully to rid them of any grit and trim off any blemishes. If you are starting with fresh or frozen black-eyed peas and cooking them, add 30 minutes to the recipe's total time. If you are using canned peas, the time remains the same. Here, a rich buttermilk dressing, used sparingly to keep the kale in the spotlight, pulls together all of the tastes of the salad.

CROUTONS

1 cup cubed corn bread, in ½-inch cubes

BUTTERMILK DRESSING

¾ cup buttermilk, preferably full fat

2 tablespoons mayonnaise, preferably Duke's

1 teaspoon Dijon mustard

1 teaspoon cider vinegar

1 tablespoon freshly squeezed lemon juice

1 scallion, white and light green parts, thinly sliced

¼ cup snipped fresh chives

1 small garlic clove, chopped into a paste

½ teaspoon kosher salt

Freshly ground black pepper

SALAD

1 cup toasted corn kernels

1 teaspoon extra-virgin olive oil

1 pound baby kale

½ cup cooked black-eyed peas, preferably from fresh or frozen, not canned

1 cup cherry or grape tomatoes, halved

TO MAKE THE CROUTONS

Preheat the oven to 275°F. Spread the corn bread on a baking sheet and bake until lightly golden and crisp, about 20 minutes. Let cool completely.

TO MAKE THE BUTTERMILK DRESSING

Combine all the ingredients in a small bowl and whisk until well blended. If not using immediately, transfer to an airtight container and refrigerate for up to 3 days.

TO MAKE THE SALAD

Heat a medium cast-iron skillet over high heat. Add the olive oil and corn and cook, stirring, until the kernels are fragrant and begin to char, about 2 minutes. Transfer to a plate to cool.

Combine the kale, cooled corn, black-eyed peas, and tomatoes in a large bowl. Add enough of the dressing to lightly coat the kale and other vegetables and toss to coat evenly. Transfer to a serving bowl, garnish with the croutons, and serve.

POTATO SALAD

❈

SERVES

6 to **8**

ACTIVE TIME
20 MINS
🕐
TOTAL TIME
3 HRS

A NATIVE OF GUYANA, SOUTH America, Dionne Alleyne is one of Sweet Home Café's senior cooks and has been a key member of the culinary team since the opening. When she was asked to create a classic southern-style potato salad, she combined her culinary passion and skill in this version, which has been a winner at the Café since it first appeared on the menu.

2 pounds Yukon Gold potatoes, uniform in size, unpeeled

3 teaspoons kosher salt, divided

¼ cup yellow onion, finely diced

¼ cup cider vinegar

2 tablespoons sugar

¾ cup mayonnaise, preferably Duke's

3 tablespoons yellow mustard

¼ cup sweet pickle relish

½ cup celery, finely diced

¼ cup fresh flat-leaf parsley, finely chopped

¼ cup scallions, white and light green parts, thinly sliced

Freshly ground black pepper

Put the potatoes and 2 teaspoons of the salt into a large pot and cover with cold water. Bring to a boil and then reduce to a simmer and cook the potatoes until tender, about 25 minutes (test by inserting the tip of a paring knife into a potato; it should be tender but still firm). Drain the potatoes and let cool in a single layer to room temperature.

Once the potatoes have cooled, carefully peel off the skins and cut the potatoes into medium dice.

Put the onion into a small strainer and rinse briefly under cold water. Pat dry on a paper towel.

In a large bowl, combine the vinegar, sugar, and remaining 1 teaspoon salt and whisk until the sugar and salt are dissolved. Then add the mayonnaise, mustard, and relish, whisking until well blended.

Add the potatoes, celery, onion, parsley, and scallions to the mayonnaise and gently mix. Refrigerate for at least 2 hours prior to serving. Once the salad is fully chilled, check the seasoning and adjust with salt and pepper to taste.

COLESLAW

CONTINENTAL
UNITED STATES

SERVES

4 to **6**

ACTIVE TIME
30 MINS
🕐
TOTAL TIME
**3 HRS
30 MINS**

THE WORD *COLESLAW* COMES from the Dutch *koolsla*, or "cabbage salad." In fact, cabbage is the only consistent ingredient in coleslaw. Additions can include shaved carrots, onions, bacon, or even pineapple. Dressings also vary widely and can range from a simple mayonnaise or sour cream to a vinaigrette. This version calls for sweet pickle relish for a touch of sweetness and Tabasco for vinegary zing.

1 head green cabbage, about 2½ pounds, core and ribs removed, and leaves thinly sliced

1 cup carrot, shredded

½ cup Vidalia or other sweet onion, finely diced

¼ cup cider vinegar

¼ cup sugar

½ teaspoon celery salt

¼ teaspoon kosher salt

1 cup mayonnaise, preferably Duke's

⅓ cup sweet pickle relish

1 ½ tablespoons Creole mustard (such as Zatarain's) or Dijon mustard

2 dashes Tabasco sauce

Freshly ground black pepper

Combine the cabbage, carrot, and onion in a large bowl and set aside.

In a small bowl, combine the vinegar, sugar, celery salt, and kosher salt and whisk until the sugar and salts are dissolved. Add the mayonnaise, relish, mustard, Tabasco sauce, and pepper to taste, whisking until well blended.

With a rubber spatula, fold the mayonnaise mixture into the cabbage mixture, mixing until the cabbage is evenly coated. Cover and refrigerate for a minimum of 3 hours prior to serving. It will keep for up to one day.

PICKLED
GULF SHRIMP

SERVES
6 to **8**

ACTIVE TIME
45 MINS
🕐
TOTAL TIME
1 DAY
REFRIGERATE
OVERNIGHT

THIS DISH OF MARINATED poached shrimp makes an impressive addition to any buffet table, but it is equally at home served on a beautiful platter as an appetizer at a sit-down supper.

CHEF'S NOTE

For the best results, use only American Gulf or Georgia White shrimp. These pickled shrimp make a great party canapé. If no fresh bay leaves are available (often found in refrigerated cases in produce section), substitute 5 dried leaves.

4 quarts cold water

⅓ cup Old Bay seasoning

1 lemon, halved

2 tablespoons kosher salt

3 pounds American Gulf or Georgia White shrimp, peeled and deveined

½ teaspoon whole allspice berries

1 teaspoon celery seeds

2 garlic cloves, chopped into a paste

½ teaspoon red pepper flakes

2½ cups extra-virgin olive oil

½ cup freshly squeezed lemon juice

¾ cup flat-leaf parsley, chopped

1 Vidalia or other sweet onion, thinly sliced

3 fresh bay leaves

6 fresh thyme sprigs

3 vine-ripened tomatoes, sliced

2 ripe avocados, sliced

Pour the water into a large pot. Add the Old Bay seasoning, lemon halves, and 1 tablespoon of the kosher salt and bring to a boil. Reduce to a simmer and cook for 5 minutes. Poach the shrimp in the simmering water until they are pink and opaque, 2 to 3 minutes. Using a slotted spoon, quickly transfer the shrimp to a colander and rinse under cold water to stop the cooking. Leave the shrimp in the colander to drain well.

Crush the allspice berries and celery seeds with the back of a knife until they are finely ground; then transfer them to a medium bowl. Add the garlic paste, red pepper flakes, olive oil, lemon juice, parsley, and the remaining 1 tablespoon of salt. Whisk until all the ingredients are fully incorporated. Stir in the onion, bay leaves, and thyme sprigs.

Place the cooked shrimp in a glass container. Pour over the marinade, cover, and refrigerate overnight.

To serve, separate the shrimp and onions from the liquid and arrange on a serving platter, garnishing with the tomato and avocado slices. Whisk the remaining marinade into an emulsion and spoon some of it over the shrimp and vegetables. Leftover shrimp can be stored in the refrigerator for up to 24 hours.

SERVES

4 to 6

ACTIVE TIME
15 MINS
🕐
TOTAL TIME
1 HR

VEGETARIAN

STEWED TOMATOES &
OKRA

OKRA IS AFRICA'S CULINARY totem. It originated on the continent and made its way around the world. Nowadays, it is a common ingredient in India, Greece, Turkey, the Middle East, South America, and the American South, where it is famously added to gumbos to thicken them. This simple dish of stewed okra and tomatoes is one of the all-purpose side dishes of African American cuisine. Although it tastes best when fresh okra, available in late summer and early fall, is used, frozen okra can be substituted other times of the year.

6 large vine-ripened tomatoes, or 3 (15-ounce) cans diced tomatoes, drained

1 tablespoon olive oil

¾ cup Vidalia or other sweet onion, diced

1 jalapeño pepper, seeded and finely diced

½ cup celery, diced

2 garlic cloves, finely chopped

1 teaspoon kosher salt

½ cup Vegetable Stock (page 201)

4 cups fresh or frozen okra, cut into ½-inch-thick rounds

Freshly ground black pepper

If using fresh tomatoes, first peel them. Fill a medium stockpot with cold water and bring to a boil. Prepare a large bowl of ice water. With a paring knife, remove the core from each tomato and cut a quarter-sized X in the skin of the tomato bottom. Place the tomatoes in the boiling water for 30 seconds, then, using a slotted spoon, transfer them to the bowl of ice water. Let cool, then gently remove the skin. Dice the peeled tomatoes. You should have 4 cups.

Heat the olive oil in a large saucepan over high heat. Add the onion and cook until tender and translucent, about 2 to 3 minutes. Add the jalapeño, celery, garlic, and salt and cook for 1 minute longer.

Now add the tomatoes and Vegetable Stock and gently simmer for 15 minutes.

Next add the okra and simmer until tender, about 25 minutes longer.

Adjust the seasoning to taste with salt and pepper before serving.

OKRA

Okra gets no respect. Long demeaned for its slime and marginalized as one of those "southern things," it is definitely a vegetable about which people have strong opinions, with lovers and haters lined up to praise its thickening abilities or decry its mucilaginous properties. The green pod is native to Africa, where it is thought to have originated in the Sahel region, which lies south of the Sahara and ranges from Mali eastward to Ethiopia. On the continent of its origin, it is prized as both a thickener and a vegetable and appears in a wide array of dishes, ranging from Egypt's *bamia*, an okra stew, to Senegal's *soupikandia*, an ancestor of Louisiana's gumbo. From Africa's midsection, the green pod made its way to Mediterranean shores and may have been first cultivated in Egypt as long ago as 2000 BC.

No one is sure exactly where, when, or how okra made its way to the Western Hemisphere, though the transference is usually credited to enslaved Africans. It probably arrived in the southern United States via the Caribbean. Thomas Jefferson reported it growing in Virginia before 1781, and planted it at Monticello in 1809. Okra was well known enough to appear in several recipes in Mary Randolph's *The Virginia Housewife: Or, Methodical Cook*, published in 1824. In southern Louisiana, the word *gumbo* tells the story of okra in its name alone, for it is a corruption of the words *chingombo* and *ochingombo*, used for the vegetable in the Bantu languages of Central Africa.

KALE SPROUTS
WITH SORGHUM & BENNE

CAFÉ SPECIAL

SERVES

4 to **6**

ACTIVE TIME
30 MINS
🕐
TOTAL TIME
30 MINS

IN SOUTH CAROLINA, SESAME seeds are known as benne, from the Wolof language of Senegal. The seeds arrived on the slave ships, and through much of the nineteenth century, they were cultivated by plantation owners as an important source of cooking oil. This dish, which was developed for a special promotion in the Café, is inspired by the traditional slow-cooked kale found on many African American tables. It coats kale sprouts with a sherry vinegar–sorghum glaze and adds caramelized shallots and garlic for their rich flavor and benne for their crunch.

CHEF'S NOTE

Look for kale sprouts, also called kalettes, in specialty markets or farm stands. If unavailable, use baby kale in their place.

8 cups cold water

1 teaspoon kosher salt

2 pounds kale sprouts, stems trimmed

2 tablespoons avocado oil

¼ cup shallots, finely sliced

4 garlic cloves, thinly sliced

2 tablespoons sherry vinegar

3 tablespoons sorghum syrup

1 tablespoon unsalted butter

2 tablespoons toasted benne (sesame) seeds

In a large soup pot, bring the water and salt to a boil. Add the kale sprouts and cook for 1 minute.

Immediately remove the pot from the stovetop, pour the contents through a colander, and quickly rinse the sprouts under cold water to stop the cooking process. Transfer the sprouts to a baking sheet lined with several layers of paper towels to absorb excess moisture.

Preheat a large sauté pan over medium heat and pour in the avocado oil. Add the shallots and garlic and sauté until lightly caramelized, about 1 to 2 minutes. Now add the kale sprouts and cook for 2 minutes, stirring regularly. Add the vinegar and sorghum, stirring well to coat the leaves with the glaze.

Remove the pan from the heat, add the butter and benne seeds, and stir until the butter has emulsified into the sorghum glaze. Serve hot.

SERVES
6 to 8

ACTIVE TIME
30 MINS
🕐
TOTAL TIME
2½ HRS

SLOW-COOKED
COLLARDS & POTLIKKER

✠

COLLARD GREENS ARE SUCH an African American classic that most people are surprised to discover that they are not from the African continent, but rather a northern European green. They are usually cooked long and low until silky smooth and tender. Be sure to rinse the greens thoroughly, as grit is often trapped in the folds of the leaves.

CHEF'S NOTE

To adapt this recipe for vegetarians, omit the ham hocks and use Vegetable Stock (page 201) in place of the water. Another alternative is to replace the ham hocks with 2 smoked turkey wings. Serve with hot corn bread for sopping up the potlikker, the tasty, vitamin-rich cooking liquid.

1 tablespoon vegetable oil

1 large yellow onion, finely diced

2 garlic cloves, finely chopped

2 smoked ham hocks

5 cups cold water

3 tablespoons cider vinegar

1 teaspoon red pepper flakes

1 teaspoon kosher salt

1 teaspoon hot sauce

½ teaspoon sugar

2 pounds collard greens

Freshly ground black pepper

Heat the oil in a large stockpot over medium heat. Add the onion and cook until translucent, about 5 minutes. Add the garlic and ham hocks and cook for 2 more minutes. Next add the water, vinegar, red pepper flakes, salt, hot sauce, and sugar. Bring to a steady simmer, lower the heat, and simmer gently for 1 hour.

Meanwhile, cut off the stems of the collards and slice out the rib that runs the length of each leaf. This should yield two large pieces from each leaf. Stack all the trimmed leaves on top of one another and then crosscut the leaves into ½-inch-wide ribbons. Transfer the collards to a large bowl with a large amount of cold water and agitate for 1 minute. Allow the water to settle for 5 minutes. Then, with a slotted spoon, remove the collards and transfer to another bowl. Change the water and repeat the process. The collards must be completely free of sand and dirt.

Add the cleaned collards to the ham hock stock and simmer until the collards are very tender, about 1 hour. Once the greens are tender, remove the ham hocks. When the hocks are cool enough to handle, peel off the skin, remove the meat from the bones, and chop the meat. Return the meat to the pot of greens.

Adjust the seasoning to taste with salt, hot sauce, and pepper before serving.

STEWED
BLACK-EYED PEAS

AGRICULTURAL
SOUTH

SERVES
6 to **8**

ACTIVE TIME
30 MINS
🕐
TOTAL TIME
1 DAY
PLUS
OVERNIGHT
SOAKING OF
THE PEAS

SOUTHERNERS BELIEVE THAT eating black-eyed peas on New Year's Day will bring them good luck and prosperity in the coming year, with the peas symbolizing coins and the usual side dish of greens representing folding money. To give this simple legume side dish a bolder flavor, use the Ham & Pork Stock on page 200 in place of the Chicken Stock. For a meat-free variation, leave out the ham hocks and substitute Vegetable Stock (page 201) for the cooking liquid.

CHEF'S NOTE

For those who don't eat pork, 2 smoked turkey wings can be substituted for the ham hocks. Serve the peas either as a side dish or as an entrée with Yellow Corn Bread (page 151) or Johnnycakes (page 149).

1 pound dried black-eyed peas

2 tablespoons peanut or canola oil

2 small or 1 large smoked ham hock

1 yellow onion, finely chopped

4 garlic cloves, finely chopped

1 green bell pepper, finely diced

1 small jalapeño pepper, seeded and finely diced

2 tablespoons tomato paste

1 (14.5-ounce) can crushed tomatoes

4 cups Chicken Stock (page 200)

3 bay leaves

THE NIGHT BEFORE

Sort through the black-eyed peas to remove any debris and stones. Place the beans in a colander and rinse under cold water. Transfer to a large soup pot and cover with cold water. The water level should reach at least 2 inches above the beans. Leave to soak overnight.

THE NEXT DAY

Drain and rinse the peas and reserve. In a large soup pot, heat the oil over medium heat, add the ham hocks, and lightly brown on all sides, about 5 minutes. Remove the hocks and reserve.

Add the onion and garlic and cook over medium heat until translucent, about 5 minutes. Add the bell pepper and jalapeño and cook for another 3 minutes. Then add the tomato paste and cook for 3 minutes more, allowing the paste to develop a rich flavor and color.

Now add the crushed tomatoes, black-eyed peas, Chicken Stock, reserved ham hocks, and bay leaves to the pot. Bring to a boil and then reduce to a gentle simmer. Cook uncovered for about 45 minutes, until the peas are tender. Skim off any froth that develops during the cooking process.

Remove the ham hocks, let cool until they can be handled, then peel off the skin and remove the meat from the bones. Roughly chop the meat, return it to the pot, heat through, and serve.

MIXED GREENS
WITH BABY TURNIPS

AGRICULTURAL
SOUTH

SERVES
6 to **8**

ACTIVE TIME
30 MINS
🕐
TOTAL TIME
1 HR

HERE IS ANOTHER VARIATION on the theme of greens. This method uses a tangy combination of mustard greens, turnip greens, and kale and includes baby turnips with their greens in the mix. Bacon gives the "mess" of greens its smoky flavor, but it can be left out if you prefer. In that case, another dash or two of hot sauce would be welcome.

CHEF'S NOTE
These greens are delicious served with their potlikker and corn bread.

2 pounds mustard greens

1 pound turnip greens

1 pound kale

2 pounds baby or small turnips (with tops left on), peeled

2 tablespoons vegetable oil

4 ounces applewood-smoked slab bacon, chopped

2 garlic cloves, finely chopped

½ cup yellow onion, finely chopped

3 cups Vegetable Stock (page 201)

1 teaspoon kosher salt

1 pinch sugar

2 or 3 dashes hot sauce

Freshly ground black pepper

Trim the tough stems and ribs from the mustard greens, turnip greens, and kale. Fill a clean kitchen sink with cold water and thoroughly wash the greens and baby turnips. Be sure they are free of any grit and dirt; if necessary, wash twice.

In a stewpot or large Dutch oven, heat the vegetable oil over medium heat. Add the bacon and brown well on all sides. Then add the garlic and onion and cook until translucent, about 3 minutes.

Add the kale, turnip, and mustard greens and cook, stirring, until the greens begin to wilt, 3 to 4 minutes. Pour in the Vegetable Stock and bring to a full simmer. Season with the salt and sugar and cook for 10 more minutes. Add the whole baby turnips with their tops and gently simmer until tender, about 10 minutes.

Adjust the seasoning with salt, hot sauce, and black pepper to taste.

SERVES
6 to **8**

ACTIVE TIME
35 MINS

🕐

TOTAL TIME
35 MINS

FRIED GREEN
TOMATOES

❈

THIS SOUTHERN CLASSIC IS typically prepared when the tomatoes are coming so fast they cannot all be served in salads or put up in sauces. The mix of Japanese *panko* (bread crumbs) and cornmeal gives the slices an extra-crispy crunch, while the Roast Tomato Aioli doubles the tomato taste.

ROAST TOMATO AIOLI

1 cup Aioli (page 202)

½ cup preserved roasted tomatoes or oil-packed sun-dried tomatoes, drained and finely chopped

2 tablespoons fresh flat-leaf parsley, chopped

FRIED GREEN TOMATOES

1½ cups vegetable oil

1 cup all-purpose flour

¾ cup buttermilk, preferably full fat

2 large eggs, beaten

¼ teaspoon hot sauce

⅔ cup yellow cornmeal

⅓ cup panko bread crumbs

1 tablespoon sugar

5 firm green tomatoes, cored, and cut into ¼-inch-thick slices

1 teaspoon kosher salt

¼ teaspoon freshly ground black pepper

TO MAKE THE ROAST TOMATO AIOLI

Combine all the ingredients in a small bowl and blend well. Cover and set aside.

TO MAKE THE FRIED GREEN TOMATOES

Pour the vegetable oil into a large cast iron skillet and preheat over medium heat.

Meanwhile, pour the flour into a small bowl. In a second small bowl, whisk together the buttermilk, eggs, and hot sauce. In a third small bowl, stir together the cornmeal, bread crumbs, and sugar.

Arrange the sliced green tomatoes on a work surface and season both sides with the salt and pepper. Dredge each tomato slice first in the flour, coating all sides, then in the buttermilk blend, coating thoroughly, and finally in the bread crumb and cornmeal mix, coating on both sides. Remove and shake off any excess cornmeal. As each slice is prepared, set it aside on a baking sheet.

Using a deep-frying thermometer, confirm the temperature of the oil has reached 375°F (maintain that temperature throughout the cooking). Working in batches, place the breaded tomatoes into the oil and fry on both sides until crisp, about 2 minutes per side.

Remove the tomatoes with a slotted spoon and transfer to a separate baking sheet lined with paper towels to drain off excess oil. Serve hot with the Roast Tomato Aioli.

CORN PUDDING

AGRICULTURAL
SOUTH

SERVES
4 to **6**

ACTIVE TIME
20 MINS
🕐
TOTAL TIME
**1 HR
10 MINS**

THE AFRICAN AMERICAN kitchen often intersects with the cooking of Native Americans. Here, a southern corn pudding is a history lesson in a casserole. It combines the British tradition of pudding making with Native American corn in a dish that is pure southern comfort food.

5 ears corn, preferably locally grown, shucked and cleaned of silk

2 tablespoons sugar

1½ teaspoons kosher salt

1 tablespoon all-purpose flour

½ teaspoon freshly grated nutmeg

1 tablespoon butter, plus 2 tablespoons, melted

½ yellow onion, very finely chopped

1 large egg, beaten

2 cups half-and-half or light cream

¼ cup cream cheese, at room temperature

Preheat the oven to 350°F.

Cut the corn kernels from the cobs and transfer to a large bowl.

Add the sugar, salt, flour, and nutmeg to the corn and mix to thoroughly combine.

Melt 1 tablespoon butter in a small sauté pan over medium heat. Add the onion and cook until translucent and tender (do not brown), about 5 minutes. Then add the onion to the corn in the bowl.

In a separate medium bowl, whisk the egg, half-and-half, cream cheese, and the 2 tablespoons melted butter until well blended. Pour the cream mixture into the bowl with the corn and onion and mix until all the ingredients are fully incorporated.

Lightly grease a 9-by-13-inch baking dish with butter. Pour the corn mixture into the prepared dish and bake for 40 to 45 minutes, until set and golden brown. Serve hot.

FRIED OKRA

�֎

AGRICULTURAL
SOUTH

SERVES
6 to **8**

ACTIVE TIME
35 MINS
🕐
TOTAL TIME
40 MINS

OKRA IS ANOTHER SOUTHERN garden staple. However, some people are not fans because of its slippery mouthfeel. But this commonly shunned vegetable often seduces when it is fried. Here, the Creole-spiced pods pick up even more taste from a dip that salutes pimento cheese, another hallmark of the southern table.

2½ pounds large okra

2 cups buttermilk

1½ tablespoons Creole Spice Blend (page 196)

2 cups cornmeal, preferably stone-ground

1½ cups all-purpose flour

1 teaspoon kosher salt

4 cups vegetable oil for frying

Trim the stem ends of the okra. Place the pods in a large bowl, add the buttermilk, and stir gently to coat evenly. In a small shallow bowl, mix the Creole Spice Blend with the cornmeal, flour, and salt.

Pour the vegetable oil into a medium, heavy-gauge pot and heat to 350°F on a deep-frying thermometer (or use a tabletop deep-fryer). Remove the okra from the buttermilk one pod at a time and toss with the cornmeal mixture, coating evenly. Set aside on a baking sheet.

Working in batches to avoid crowding, add the okra to the hot oil and fry until golden and crispy, 6 to 7 minutes. Using a slotted spoon, transfer the fried okra to a platter lined with paper towels to absorb excess oil. Keep warm. Repeat until all the okra is fried.

Serve the okra hot with Pimento Cheese Aioli (recipe below) as a dipping sauce.

PIMENTO CHEESE AIOLI

¾ cup Pimento Cheese (page 139)

1 cup Aioli (page 202)

1 pinch cayenne pepper

1 dash Worcestershire sauce

Put the Pimento Cheese in the bowl of a food processor and blend until smooth. Transfer to a medium bowl. With a rubber spatula, fold in the Aioli and season with the cayenne and Worcestershire sauce. Refrigerate until serving.

SERVES
8 to 10

ACTIVE TIME
20 MINS

TOTAL TIME
1 HR

GINGER & BROWN SUGAR CANDIED
SWEET POTATOES

FOR MANY PEOPLE, IT IS NOT Thanksgiving without a casserole dish of candied sweet potatoes—often incorrectly called candied yams—placed prominently on the table. (The yam, an edible tropical tuber, belongs to a different botanical family.) This version has so much taste that you won't even miss the marshmallows.

6 sweet potatoes
(about 4½ pounds)

1 pinch kosher salt,
plus 2 teaspoons

1 cup freshly squeezed
orange juice

¾ cup packed light
brown sugar

½ cup (1 stick) unsalted butter

4 tablespoons grated
peeled fresh ginger

½ vanilla bean, or ½ teaspoon
pure vanilla extract

2 cinnamon sticks

1 teaspoon freshly
grated nutmeg

Peel the sweet potatoes and cut into ¾-inch-thick slices. Put them in a pot, cover with cold water, and add the pinch of salt. Bring the water to a boil, reduce to a simmer, and cook for 5 minutes.

While the sweet potatoes simmer, put all the remaining ingredients in a small saucepan and bring to a boil over medium heat. The ingredients should blend into a creamy consistency. Remove from the heat and set aside. Preheat the oven to 325°F.

Drain the sweet potatoes. Transfer them to a 9-by-13-inch baking dish and pour over the orange juice mixture. Gently mix to coat the sweet potatoes.

Bake uncovered for about **40 minutes,** until the liquid has thickened and the sweet potatoes are tender and glazed. Gently stir the potatoes two or three times during the cooking process to help thicken the glaze. Serve hot.

YANKEE
BAKED BEANS

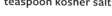

NORTHERN
STATES

SERVES

6 to 8

ACTIVE TIME
40 MINS
🕐
TOTAL TIME
1 DAY
PLUS
OVERNIGHT
SOAKING OF
THE BEANS

YANKEE BAKED BEANS, SOME-times called Boston baked beans, were common New England fare by the mid-seventeenth century. Traditionally cooked low and slow in a stoneware pot on a wood-fired stove—a technique mimicked with today's slow cookers—they were a go-to dish served everywhere from lumber camps to fancy restaurants, often on Saturday night. Molasses, the residue left over from sugar refining, is the common sweetener except in Vermont, where maple syrup is typically used. This version uses two sweeteners, molasses and maple sugar.

1 pound dried great northern beans

1 small yellow onion, peeled but left whole, plus 1 cup finely diced yellow onion

1 large carrot, peeled

1 celery stalk

⅓ cup unsulfured molasses

2 tablespoons maple sugar

⅓ cup packed light brown sugar

1 teaspoon kosher salt

3 tablespoons Dijon mustard

2 bay leaves

1 pinch ground cloves

8 ounces salt pork or bacon slab, cut into 1-inch cubes

2 teaspoons freshly ground black pepper

2 dashes cider vinegar (optional)

THE NIGHT BEFORE

Sort through the beans to remove any debris and stones. Place the beans in a colander and rinse under cold water. Transfer to a large soup pot and cover with cold water. The water level should reach at least 2 inches above the beans. Leave to soak overnight.

THE NEXT DAY

Drain the beans, rinse with cold water, and add fresh water to 2 inches below top of pot. Add the whole onion, carrot, and celery. Place the beans over medium heat and cook uncovered at a steady simmer until creamy and tender, about 45 minutes. Drain the beans through a colander, reserving half of the cooking water, and keeping the beans and cooking water separate. Discard the onion, carrot, and celery.

Preheat the oven to 325°F.

In a medium bowl, combine the molasses, maple sugar, brown sugar, salt, mustard, bay leaves, and cloves with 1 cup of the reserved bean cooking water. Stir until fully blended.

Put the beans, salt pork, diced onion, and the molasses mixture in a heavy pot with a fitted lid (such as a Dutch oven) and mix well. Bake, stirring every 30 minutes, until tender, 4 to 5 hours. If the beans begin to look dry before they are ready, add about ½ cup of the reserved bean cooking water to moisten them. To develop a rich browning, the cooking liquid should come just to the top of the beans but not fully cover them.

When the beans are done, remove them from the oven and stir well. Adjust the seasoning with salt and pepper to taste. You can also adjust the level of tartness with a splash or two of cider vinegar.

BAKED
MACARONI & CHEESE

SERVES

4 to **6**

ACTIVE TIME
30 MINS
⊘
TOTAL TIME
**1 HR
10 MINS**

FOOD HISTORIANS DEBATE whether Thomas Jefferson brought home a recipe for macaroni and cheese from England or from northern Italy. No one knows. What we do know is that a variant of the dish was served at a state dinner in 1802 and mentioned in reports as "a pie called macaroni." A variation of this dish appears in *The Virginia Housewife: Or, Methodical Cook*, an 1824 cookbook by Mary Randolph, a cousin of Jefferson's. Whatever its origin, the dish has been taken to the hearts and stomachs of African Americans in the United States and in the Caribbean, where it is sometimes known by its British name, macaroni pie. This version uses Cheddar, though some cooks use other cheeses.

4 tablespoons unsalted butter

½ cup all-purpose flour

1 cup whole milk

3 cups half-and-half

1 teaspoon dry English mustard

⅛ teaspoon freshly grated nutmeg

1 pinch cayenne pepper

2 teaspoons kosher salt

Freshly ground black pepper

12 ounces sharp orange Cheddar cheese, grated, divided

1 pound elbow macaroni, cooked and drained

Preheat the oven to 325°F. Lightly butter a 9-by-13-inch broiler-proof baking dish.

In a large saucepan over low heat, melt the butter. Add the flour and stir with a wooden spoon until smooth. Increase the heat to medium and cook, stirring, until the mixture turns a light golden color, about 3 minutes. Whisk in the milk and half-and-half, then bring to a simmer while continuing to whisk. Simmer the sauce for about 5 minutes, until nicely thickened. Remove from the heat.

Stir in the mustard, nutmeg, cayenne, salt, and pepper to taste, followed by three-quarters of the grated cheese. Whisk until all the ingredients are fully incorporated. Add the cooked macaroni to the cheese sauce and toss to blend.

Pour the macaroni mixture into the prepared baking dish. Bake for 30 minutes, until the mac and cheese is bubbly. Top with the remaining cheese. Reset the oven to the broiler setting and broil until the cheese has slightly blistered and is lightly browned. Serve hot.

SERVES

4 to 6

ACTIVE TIME
20 MINS
🕐
TOTAL TIME
1 DAY
PLUS
OVERNIGHT
SOAKING OF
THE PEAS

HOPPIN' JOHN

IF IT IS NEW YEAR'S DAY AND a southerner is in the kitchen—or even in the room—there will probably be some Hoppin' John on the table. Native to South Carolina's Low Country, this humble dish of black-eyed peas and rice cooked together, a method brought from Africa, has its culinary kin in the red beans and rice of Louisiana and the *moros y cristianos* (black beans and rice) of Cuba. On New Year's Day, Hoppin' John symbolizes good luck. The rest of the year, it simply tastes good.

CHEF'S NOTE

Sea Island Red Peas, small red peas long grown in the Sea Islands off the South Carolina coast, are traditionally paired with Carolina Gold rice in Hoppin' John.

1 cup dried black-eyed peas or Sea Island Red Peas

4 cups Ham & Pork Stock (page 200)

2 bay leaves

4 thick bacon slices, diced

1 onion, minced

1 garlic clove, finely chopped

1 celery stalk, finely diced

1 green bell pepper, finely diced

1 cup Carolina Gold rice

1½ teaspoons kosher salt

¾ teaspoon freshly ground black pepper

¼ bunch fresh flat-leaf parsley, chopped

4 scallions, white and light green parts, thinly sliced

THE NIGHT BEFORE

Sort through the black-eyed peas to remove any debris and stones. Place the peas in a colander and rinse under cold water. Transfer to a medium soup pot and cover with cold water. The water level should reach at least 2 inches above the peas. Leave to soak overnight.

THE NEXT DAY

Drain the black-eyed peas and rinse with cold water.

Combine the peas, Ham & Pork Stock, and bay leaves in the soup pot and bring to a simmer uncovered. Cook uncovered until the peas are tender but not mushy, 45 minutes to 1 hour.

Drain the peas, reserving both the peas and the stock. Discard the bay leaves.

Rinse the soup pot and return it to the stovetop. Add the bacon and cook over medium heat to render the fat. Once the bacon is crisp, remove it with a slotted spoon and set aside, leaving the fat in the pot.

Add the onion and garlic to the pot and cook over medium heat until translucent, about 5 minutes. Then add the celery and bell pepper and cook for another 3 minutes. Stir in the rice, salt, pepper, and 2½ cups of the reserved Ham & Pork Stock. Cover and simmer over low heat until the rice is tender, 18 to 20 minutes.

When the rice is done, stir in the crisp bacon, peas, parsley, and scallions and serve.

RICE

Most of us are unaware that the African continent has its own species of rice, *Oryza glaberrima*. Yet for many on the western coast of the African continent, rice is the staff of life and the center of agricultural pursuit. Indeed, in the times when the African coastline was named for its major exports (Ivory, Gold, and even Slave), the area that stretches from southern Senegal to Liberia was known as the Rice Coast. The enslaved carried their knowledge of rice growing with them and were important in the development of a system that transformed the agriculture of the New World. Not surprisingly, European slavers valued this wisdom, and slaves from the Rice Coast commanded higher prices.

Ethnobotanists today are discovering that enslaved Africans may have been responsible for more than widely disseminating knowledge of rice culture. One or more of the originally grown strains were possibly West African cultivars, though they were later replaced by the Asian rice species that are cultivated today.

People from the Rice Coast also carried many rice recipes from Africa to the Americas. Dishes such as Hoppin' John, red rice, and Limpin' Susan share ties with West African cooking, telling the history of both a grain and a people on the plate.

Stereographs of rice cultivation and transportation in South Carolina, late nineteenth to early twentieth century.

SERVES
4 to 6

ACTIVE TIME
10 MINS

🕐

TOTAL TIME
40 MINS

RICE PILAF

COASTAL SOUTH CAROLINA was the center of rice cultivation in America in the seventeenth century, and more than three centuries later, kitchens along the Creole Coast continue to celebrate this historic grain in an amazing array of dishes. In South Carolina, these rice dishes, or pilafs, are known as purloos or pilaus. All three terms come from the Turkish *pilav*, which in turn is borrowed from the Persian *polow*.

CHEF'S NOTE

The Café uses Carolina Gold rice, prized for its superior flavor, texture, and aroma and now grown in the Carolinas, Georgia, and Texas, for this dish, but any high-quality long-grain white rice can be substituted.

2 tablespoons butter

½ yellow onion, finely chopped

2 cups Carolina Gold rice

3¼ cups Chicken Stock (page 200)

1 bay leaf

Preheat the oven to 350°F.

In a wide, heavy-bottomed, ovenproof medium pot with a lid, melt the butter over medium heat. Add the onion and cook until translucent, about 5 minutes.

Add the rice and stir well to coat the grains with the butter. Cook, stirring, until the rice develops a slight nutty aroma, about 2 to 3 minutes. Do not let it brown.

Add the Chicken Stock and bay leaf, bring to a boil, and give the rice one final stir. Place the lid on the pot and immediately transfer to the oven. Bake for 15 minutes. Remove the pot, leaving the lid on, and let rest undisturbed for 10 to 15 minutes. Remove the bay leaf and serve.

RICE & PIGEON PEAS

CULINARY
COUSINS

SERVES

4 to 6

ACTIVE TIME
20 MINS
🕐
TOTAL TIME
**1 HR
10 MINS**

THIS DISH, BELOVED THROUGH-out the Caribbean and Central America, is called peas and rice everywhere except Jamaica, where it is called rice and peas. (The Jamaicans argue that there is more rice than peas!) Pigeon peas, also known as gungo peas, *pois congos*, or *gandules*, originated in India, and remnants have been found in archaeological sites that date back thirty-five hundred years. They migrated to the African continent and arrived in the Americas in the seventeenth century with the transatlantic slave trade. In Puerto Rico, a variation of this dish is served at Christmas.

CHEF'S NOTE

This dish is delicious served with Curried Goat (page 119) or Jamaican Jerk Chicken (page 101).

12 cups Chicken Stock (page 200)

½ cup coconut milk

1 (15½-ounce) can pigeon peas, rinsed and drained

2 teaspoons fresh thyme leaves

½ teaspoon ground allspice

2 scallions, white and light green parts, thinly sliced

½ cup minced yellow onion

3 garlic cloves, minced

1 Scotch bonnet or jalapeño pepper, uncut, washed

1 teaspoon packed light brown sugar

2¼ cups long-grain white rice

1½ teaspoons kosher salt

1 teaspoon freshly ground black pepper

In a stockpot, combine the Chicken Stock, coconut milk, and peas and bring to a boil over high heat. Cover the pot, reduce the heat to low, and simmer for 20 minutes, until the peas are tender and creamy.

Add the thyme, allspice, scallions, onion, garlic, Scotch bonnet pepper, brown sugar, rice, salt, and pepper. There should be at least 1 inch of liquid covering the rice. If not, add water or more Chicken Stock.

Bring to a boil over high heat, reduce the heat to low, cover, and simmer for 20 to 30 minutes, until rice is tender. Remove the Scotch bonnet pepper prior to serving.

LOUIS ARMSTRONG'S
RED BEANS & RICE

CREOLE COAST

SERVES
6

ACTIVE TIME
45 MINS
🕐
TOTAL TIME
5 HRS
PLUS
OVERNIGHT
SOAKING OF
THE BEANS

RED BEANS AND RICE IS A classic Monday-night dinner in New Orleans. Monday was traditionally washday, and the cook could put a pot on the stove to cook slowly while the washing was done. Louis Armstrong was such a fan of the dish that he signed his letters "red beans and ricely yours." His family recipe, a typewritten version of which is in his archives at Queens College in New York City, uses tomato sauce, which is not an ingredient in the traditional recipe.

CHEF'S NOTE

If pork is off your menu, you can substitute chicken fat for the salt pork and corned beef or tongue for the ham hock. This is Louis Armstrong's family recipe as originally published.

BEANS

1 pound dried kidney beans

8 ounces salt pork, or
2 slab bacon slices

6 small ham hocks,
or 1 smoked pork butt

2 yellow onions, diced

¼ green bell pepper, diced

1 garlic clove, chopped

1 large or 2 medium
dried hot peppers

Salt

1 (6-ounce) can tomato sauce
(optional)

RICE

2 cups white rice

3 cups cold water

1 teaspoon salt

TO MAKE THE BEANS

Wash the beans thoroughly, then cover with cold water and soak overnight. When ready to cook, pour the water off the beans, put them in a large pot, and add fresh water to cover. Add the salt pork or bacon. Cover the pot and bring to a boil over high heat. Reduce the heat to a simmer and cook for 1½ hours. Add the onions, bell pepper, garlic, dried peppers, and salt to taste and cook for 3 more hours. Stir in the tomato sauce (if using), then cook 1½ hours more, adding water as needed. The beans and meat should always be just covered with liquid; don't let the mixture get dry.

To prepare with ham hocks or pork butt, wash the meat, add water to cover, and bring to a boil in a covered pot over medium heat. Cook for 1½ hours. Then add the presoaked beans (first pour the water off) and the remaining ingredients. Cook for 4½ hours. Add water as needed.

TO MAKE THE RICE

Rinse the rice thoroughly under cold running water.

Bring the water and salt to a boil in a medium saucepan. Add the rice to the boiling water. Cook until the rice swells and the water is almost evaporated. Then cover, turn the heat to low, and cook until the rice is grainy. To ensure grainy rice, use 1½ cups water to 1 cup rice.

SOUPS

AND

STEWS

Bottom: *Hot crab pot*, 1979; printed 2007. Photograph by Jeanne Moutoussamy-Ashe.

Opposite, top right: A group dining in Hunt's Cafe in Earle, Arkansas, early to mid-twentieth century.

Opposite, bottom right: Comparing root vegetables at a Harlem, New York, grocery store, ca. 1959. Photograph by Lloyd W. Yearwood.

SOUPS
AND
STEWS

Feature: Western Range / 56

Frogmore Stew / 59

Chesapeake Corn & Crab Chowder / 60

Collard, Tomato, & Cashew Stew / 61

Duck & Crawfish Gumbo / 62

Okra & Tomato Soup / 64

Cowpea & Collard Soup / 65

Son-of-a-Gun Stew / 67

Brunswick Stew / 68

"Smoking Hot" Oxtail Pepper Pot / 69

Feature: Peanuts / 70

Senegalese Peanut Soup / 71

WESTERN RANGE

Whether in Denver or Dallas, St. Louis or San Francisco, the adventurous spirit has prevailed in the western section of the country, where many African Americans settled in the aftermath of the Civil War. As this new frontier was opening, those in search of a different, better life headed west to seek their fortune. From the cowboys and chuck-wagon cooks who deployed their skills at roping and wrangling, and their cast iron skillets, to the intrepid black prospectors who worked mining claims and the brave buffalo soldiers who patrolled the range, to the citizens of Tulsa, Oklahoma's Black Wall Street, African Americans had a hand in shaping life in the western states and left their culinary mark wherever they stopped.

In the West, African Americans continued to make fortunes in food service. Barney Ford, a thwarted gold rush prospector turned barber turned restaurateur, eventually built a hotel in Denver that featured a seven-page menu in French and English and served dishes such as trout, oysters, and game to the city's new silver millionaires.

Abby Fisher was a former slave whose journeys eventually led her to San Francisco and a career in catering and pickle making. In 1881, her delighted customers helped her to pen a tome called *What Mrs. Fisher Knows about Old Southern Cooking: Soups, Pickles, Preserves, Etc.*, which, for many years, was considered the first African American cookbook. In the same city, Mary Ellen Pleasant, another former southerner, ended up as a boarding house (some say brothel) owner. She listened at the table as her patrons spoke of their business deals, invested along with them, and eventually not only grew her own sizable fortune but also led the march toward equality, becoming known as San Francisco's "Mother of Civil Rights in California."

The tradition of catering was continued into the twentieth century by, among others, Cleora Butler of Tulsa, whose business spanned decades and whose 1985 cookbook, *Cleora's Kitchens: The Memoir of a Cook & Eight Decades of Great American Food*, is a virtual history of African American entertaining.

Above: The galley kitchen of a railroad dining car, early to mid-twentieth century.

Opposite, top right: *Loading the "Chuck" Wagon*, ca. 1906. Created by Charles E. Morris.

Opposite, bottom right: Carafe used by the Pullman Palace Car Company, mid-twentieth century.

TEXAS CAVIAR

Loading the "Chuck" Wagon

M 401

JOHNNYCAKES

PULLMAN

FROGMORE STEW

CREOLE COAST

SERVES
8

ACTIVE TIME
40 MINS

🕐

TOTAL TIME
1 HR

ALSO KNOWN AS BEAUFORT stew or a Low Country boil, this dish is one of the many seafood boils popular in the coastal areas of South Carolina and Georgia. It is named for Frogmore, the traditional mailing address for Saint Helena Island in the Sea Islands, just off the South Carolina coast. The mix of seafood, corn, and sausage is usually cooked in large quantities and is a perfect excuse for a summer party.

CHEF'S NOTE
The Café uses Georgia coastal shrimp for true local flavor.

8 quarts cold water

1 cup Old Bay seasoning

¼ cup kosher salt

4 tomatoes, quartered

2 yellow onions, quartered

1 celery stalk

1 lemon, quartered, plus wedges for serving

2 pounds small new potatoes, preferably Red Bliss or Yukon Gold

1 pound high-quality kielbasa or other smoked sausage, cut into 2-inch pieces

36 large shrimp in the shell

8 live large blue crabs

8 ears fresh corn, shucked, cleaned of silk, and halved crosswise

Cocktail sauce, for serving

Unsalted butter, for serving

In a large stockpot (at least 16-quart capacity), bring the water to a rolling boil. Add the Old Bay seasoning, salt, tomatoes, onions, celery, and lemon. Reduce the heat to a simmer and cook for 15 minutes.

Add the potatoes and sausage and cook for 10 minutes longer.

Next add the shrimp, crabs, and corn and simmer for another 7 minutes.

Drain off the liquid through a colander. Transfer the stew to a serving platter and serve immediately, accompanied with lemon wedges, a favorite cocktail sauce, and butter.

CHESAPEAKE
CORN & CRAB
CHOWDER

SERVES
6

ACTIVE TIME
35 MINS

TOTAL TIME
1 HR
5 MINS

CHESAPEAKE CORN CHOWDER, a culinary cousin of the clam chowder of New England, show-cases not only its namesake corn, a popular local crop, but also the bounty of the bay.

CHEF'S NOTE
Check ingredients needed for the Crab Stock recipe (page 199) prior to grocery shopping. Serve this creamy soup with oyster crackers or corn bread croutons.

3 tablespoons butter

1 cup minced yellow onion

2 garlic cloves, finely chopped

3 celery stalks, finely diced

3 leeks, white and light green parts, washed well and finely diced

1 small carrot, peeled, finely diced

1½ tablespoons all-purpose flour

1 tablespoon Old Bay seasoning

4 cups Crab Stock (page 199)

4 Yukon Gold potatoes, peeled and chopped

4 cups fresh local Silver Queen corn kernels, (from 10 or 12 ears) or thawed frozen corn kernels

2 bay leaves

2 fresh thyme sprigs

1 cup heavy cream

1 pound jumbo lump crabmeat, picked over for shell bits

2 teaspoons kosher salt

Freshly ground black pepper

¼ cup fresh flat-leaf parsley, chopped

1 tablespoon fresh chives, snipped

In a large soup pot over medium heat, melt the butter. Add the onion and garlic and cook until translucent, about 5 minutes. Add the celery, leeks, and carrot and cook for another 3 minutes.

Sprinkle the flour over the vegetables and stir until the vegetables are well coated. Cook for 3 minutes longer, stirring continually. Stir in the Old Bay seasoning.

Add the Crab Stock and bring to a boil. Reduce the heat to a simmer, add the potatoes, and cook for 12 minutes. Remove 2 cups of the chowder (be sure to include a mixture of vegetables and potatoes) and transfer to a blender. Puree until smooth and thick. Return the puree to the soup pot. Add the corn kernels, bay leaves, and thyme and cook for 10 minutes longer.

Add the cream and crabmeat to the pot and simmer for 5 minutes. Season with the salt and pepper, then taste and adjust the seasoning if needed. Just prior to serving, stir in the parsley and chives.

COLLARD, TOMATO,
& CASHEW STEW

CAFÉ SPECIAL

SERVES
4 to **6**

ACTIVE TIME
50 MINS
🕐
TOTAL TIME
**1 HR
30 MINS**

VEGETARIAN

IN THIS INSPIRED MIX OF boldly flavored ingredients, ginger, cardamom pods, and curry powder join forces with collard greens, cashew nuts, and coconut milk to create a savory taste that evokes both Africa and Asia. Serve this dish over a bed of rice.

2 tablespoons peanut or canola oil

¾ cup cashew halves

½ cup minced yellow onion

3 garlic cloves, finely chopped

1½ tablespoons finely grated peeled fresh ginger

½ teaspoon smoked paprika

1 teaspoon curry powder

1 jalapeño pepper, seeded and minced

1 tablespoon tomato paste

3 cups Vegetable Stock (page 201)

6 cardamom pods, lightly cracked

2 bay leaves

¼ cup oil-packed sun-dried tomatoes, drained and chopped

½ cup crushed tomatoes

2 large sweet potatoes, peeled and cut into large dice

¾ teaspoon sea salt

¼ teaspoon freshly ground black pepper

2 bunches collard greens, stems and ribs removed, cut into ¼-inch-wide ribbons, and well washed (see Collards & Potlikker, page 34)

¾ cup coconut milk

¼ cup creamy organic cashew butter

3 tablespoons fresh cilantro, coarsely chopped, for garnish

3 scallions, white and light green parts, thinly sliced, for garnish

Heat a large soup pot over medium-low heat. Add the peanut oil, then add the cashews and cook for 2 to 3 minutes, until a nutty aroma has developed.

Add the onion, garlic, and ginger and cook for 5 minutes longer. Stir in the paprika, curry powder, and jalapeño, mixing well.

Add the tomato paste and cook, stirring often, for 3 to 4 minutes, until it lightly caramelizes. Now add the Vegetable Stock, cardamom, bay leaves, sun-dried tomatoes, crushed tomatoes, sweet potatoes, salt, and pepper. Bring to a simmer and cook for 8 minutes.

Add the collards and simmer for 25 minutes longer. Then add the coconut milk and continue to cook for 10 more minutes.

Stir in the cashew butter and adjust the seasoning to taste. Garnish with the cilantro and scallions.

SERVES
6 to 8

ACTIVE TIME
1 HR
🕐
TOTAL TIME
3½ HRS

DUCK & CRAWFISH
GUMBO

IN SOUTHERN LOUISIANA, there are as many different gumbos as there are grandmothers. This one is a variation on a classic Cajun duck and andouille gumbo, complete with mahogany roux.

CHEF'S NOTE

The Café uses andouille sausage, Rohan duck, and American farm-raised crawfish.

6 duck legs (about 4 pounds)

4 tablespoons Creole Spice Blend (page 196), divided

1 pound andouille sausage, cut into ½-inch-thick rounds

¼ cup all-purpose flour

¼ cup tomato paste

1 cup diced yellow onion

½ cup diced red bell pepper

½ cup diced green bell pepper

3 garlic cloves, finely chopped

6 cups Chicken Stock (page 200)

1 cup tomato puree

1 teaspoon dried oregano

2 bay leaves

½ bunch fresh thyme

¾ cup finely diced celery

2 cups okra, cut into ½-inch-thick rounds

1 tablespoon unsalted butter

1 cup cooked crawfish tails

1 tablespoon gumbo filé powder

Salt

Freshly ground black pepper

Tabasco sauce (optional)

Steamed white rice, for serving

Arrange the duck legs on a baking sheet and season by rubbing all sides well with 2 tablespoons of the Creole Spice Blend. Let the duck sit at room temperature for 20 minutes.

Heat a large, heavy-bottomed stewpot or Dutch oven (cast iron is excellent for gumbo) over medium heat. Place the duck legs skin-side down in the pot, and allow the fat to render from the duck. Reduce the heat to low. Brown the skin side well for 30 minutes, then turn and brown the flesh side for a further 10 minutes. Avoid burning the duck fat. Once the duck is browned but not fully cooked, remove the legs and transfer to a platter. Next brown the sausage in the duck fat in the same pot. Remove the sausage but leave the fat in the pan.

Make a roux by adding the flour to the duck fat and cooking over low heat until it turns a rich chocolate brown, about 8 to 10 minutess. Be sure to stir the roux often to keep it from burning. Once the roux has browned, immediately add the tomato paste, stir well, and cook for 2 minutes. Then add the onion, red and green bell peppers, and garlic and cook for 3 more minutes while stirring regularly.

Whisk the Chicken Stock and tomato puree into the roux, mixing well. Increase the heat and bring to a simmer, enabling the stock to thicken. Add the duck legs, sausage, the remaining 2 tablespoons Creole Spice Blend, oregano, bay leaves, thyme, and celery and simmer for 1½ hours. During this cooking time, regularly skim off excess fat from the surface.

Carefully remove the duck from the pot and set aside to cool slightly. Then remove and discard the skin. Cut the meat from the bones into about 1-inch cubes. Discard the bones, return the meat to the pot, and cook for an additional 10 minutes. Add the okra and cook for 10 more minutes, until tender.

In a medium skillet over high heat, melt the butter and allow it to lightly brown. Quickly add the cooked crawfish tails and sauté for 2 minutes. Add the crawfish to the gumbo and stir in the filé powder. Remove the bay leaves. Taste and adjust the seasoning with salt and pepper and with Tabasco sauce if you like it hotter. Serve over rice.

SERVES

6 to 8

ACTIVE TIME
30 MINS
🕐
TOTAL TIME
**1 HR
30 MINS**

OKRA &
TOMATO SOUP

THIS ALL-SEASON SOUP CAN be made from fresh ingredients in high summer when tomatoes and okra are at their peak, or from frozen okra and canned tomatoes (or better, home-preserved ones) in the cold winter months.

6 large vine-ripened tomatoes, or 1 (28-ounce) can whole peeled tomatoes, seeded and roughly chopped, with juices

3 bacon slices, finely chopped

1 cup yellow onion, finely chopped

1 celery stalk, finely diced

6 garlic cloves, finely chopped

2 tablespoons tomato paste

½ teaspoon smoked paprika

1 pound okra, cut into ¾-inch-thick rounds

2 fresh thyme sprigs

¼ teaspoon red pepper flakes

6 cups Chicken Stock (page 200)

2 bay leaves

1½ teaspoons kosher salt

¼ teaspoon freshly ground black pepper

1½ tablespoons fresh flat-leaf parsley, finely chopped, for garnish

If using fresh tomatoes, first peel them. Fill a medium stockpot with cold water and bring to a boil. Prepare a large bowl of ice water. With a paring knife, remove the core from each tomato and cut a quarter-sized X in the skin of the tomato bottom. Place the tomatoes in the boiling water for 30 seconds, then, using a slotted spoon, transfer them to the bowl of ice water. Let cool, then gently remove the skin. Roughly chop the peeled tomatoes. You should have 4 cups.

In a large soup pot over medium heat, fry the bacon until the fat renders and the bacon is crisp, about 3 to 5 minutes.

Add the onion, celery, and garlic and cook until translucent, about 5 minutes. Then add the tomato paste and cook over low heat for 5 more minutes, stirring regularly, until the paste is lightly caramelized. Add the paprika, okra, thyme, and red pepper flakes and cook for 10 minutes, until okra is tender.

Add the tomatoes, Chicken Stock, bay leaves, salt, and pepper and simmer uncovered for 30 minutes. Remove the bay leaves. Garnish with the parsley just before serving.

COWPEA
& COLLARD SOUP

AGRICULTURAL
SOUTH

SERVES
6 to **8**

ACTIVE TIME
30 MINS

TOTAL TIME
1 DAY
PLUS
OVERNIGHT
SOAKING OF
THE PEAS

TWO AFRICAN AMERICAN staples, the cowpea, a general term that includes black-eyed peas, crowder peas, and more, and dark green, leafy collard greens, are combined in this old-school recipe. Serve this warming soup when the chilly autumn air begins to blow.

CHEF'S NOTE

For those who don't eat pork, smoked turkey wings can be substituted for the ham hocks.

2 cups dried cowpeas

¼ cup canola oil

1 pound smoked ham hock

1 cup yellow onion, finely chopped

3 garlic cloves, finely chopped

2 celery stalks, finely diced

2 leeks, white and light green parts, well washed and thinly sliced

2 carrots, peeled and finely diced

¼ teaspoon smoked paprika

6 cups Chicken Stock (page 200)

2 bay leaves

1½ teaspoons sea salt

¾ teaspoon freshly ground black pepper

⅛ teaspoon cayenne pepper

2 bunches collard greens, stems and ribs removed, cut into ¼-inch-wide ribbons, and well washed (see Collards & Potlikker, page 34)

THE NIGHT BEFORE

Sort through the cowpeas to remove any debris and stones. Place the cowpeas in a colander and rinse under cold water. Transfer to a large soup pot and cover with cold water. The water level should reach at least 2 inches above the cowpeas. Leave to soak overnight.

THE NEXT DAY

Drain the cowpeas, rinse with cold water, and set aside.

In the large soup pot, heat the canola oil. Add the ham hock and brown it on all sides. Then add the onion and garlic and cook until translucent, about 5 minutes. Add the celery, leeks, carrots, and paprika and cook for 5 more minutes.

Add the Chicken Stock, cowpeas, bay leaves, salt, pepper, and cayenne and simmer for about 45 minutes, until the cowpeas are tender. Then add the collards and simmer for another 20 minutes, until the collards are tender.

Remove the ham hock, peel off the skin, and remove the meat from the bones. Chop the meat, return it to the pot, and heat through before serving.

SON-OF-A-GUN
STEW

WESTERN
RANGE

SERVES

4 to **6**

ACTIVE TIME
50 MINS

TOTAL TIME
**2 HRS
50 MINS**

IT IS OFTEN FORGOTTEN that a significant number of American cowboys were African American and that some of them became camp cooks. Originally, this stew was a special treat that was only prepared after an animal had been slaughtered. Brain, neck, liver, and onions, the latter known as "skunk eggs" on the trail, went into the pot. The Café's homage is less exotic and uses only beef short ribs.

CHEF'S NOTE

Ask a butcher to fully trim the short ribs of excess fat and cut them into 2- to 3-inch pieces to ensure generous portions. Veal Stock (page 201) is important to achieve the desired result, but if unavailable, substitute store-bought low-sodium beef broth.

4 pounds boneless beef short ribs, cut into 2- to 3-inch pieces

Salt

Freshly ground black pepper

½ cup all-purpose flour

2 tablespoons olive oil

4 tablespoons butter

1 large yellow onion, cut into large dice

1 carrot, peeled and cut into large dice

2 celery stalks, cut into large dice

2 tablespoons tomato paste

¾ cup red wine, preferably Cabernet

6 cups Veal Stock (page 201) or low-sodium beef broth

2 bay leaves

2 turnips, peeled and cut into large dice

2 Yukon Gold potatoes, peeled and cut into large dice

1 cup fresh corn kernels (from 1 to 2 ears)

½ cup oil-packed sun-dried tomatoes, drained and roughly chopped

¾ cup cooked pearl barley

1 tablespoon fresh thyme leaves

Preheat the oven to 350°F.

Place the short ribs on a baking sheet and season all sides with salt and pepper. Then dust the ribs with the flour until they are well coated.

Warm the olive oil and butter in a large, heavy, deep ovenproof pan over medium-high heat. Add the short ribs and brown on all sides. Remove the ribs from the pan and reserve.

Add the onion, carrot, and celery to the same pan and cook over medium heat until well caramelized, about 10 minutes. Add the tomato paste and cook for another 3 minutes, stirring often, until a rich color and aroma have developed. Add the red wine, bring it to a simmer, and cook until the liquid is reduced by half. Return the ribs to the pan and simmer for 2 more minutes.

Now add the Veal Stock and bay leaves and bring back to a simmer. Cover, transfer to the oven, and bake until the short ribs are tender, about 1 hour and 20 minutes. Using a slotted spoon, transfer the ribs to a casserole. Leave the oven on. Strain the braising liquid through a fine-mesh strainer into a saucepan. Bring to a simmer and cook for about 20 minutes, until reduced to a sauce consistency. Throughout the simmering, skim off the excess fat.

While the sauce is simmering, cook the turnips and potatoes in boiling salted water for 5 minutes. At that point they should be about three-quarters cooked. Remove them from the heat.

Add the corn, sun-dried tomatoes, potatoes, turnips, and barley to the ribs in the casserole. Top with the finished sauce and thyme. Cover and bake in the 350°F oven for 20 minutes, until the vegetables are tender, then serve.

SERVES

8

ACTIVE TIME
45 MINS

TOTAL TIME
**2 HRS
15 MINS**

BRUNSWICK
STEW

BRUNSWICK STEW, A RICH, soupy tomato-based stew claimed by both Georgia and Virginia, seems to have originated as a hunter's dish. The Virginia variant is more chicken based, and the Georgia recipe puts the accent on rabbit. In truth, any number of small mammals might make an appearance, including squirrel and possum. The Café's version uses chicken and rabbit. If rabbit is difficult to obtain, double the quantity of chicken thighs. Serve the stew with hot corn bread.

8 chicken thighs (about 2½ pounds)

1 whole rabbit (2½ to 3 pounds)

1 tablespoon kosher salt

1 teaspoon freshly ground black pepper

6 bacon slices, finely chopped

4 tablespoons unsalted butter, divided

1 yellow onion, finely diced

½ cup crushed tomatoes

2 bay leaves

1 fresh thyme sprig

4 cups Chicken Stock (page 200)

1 pound Yukon Gold potatoes, peeled and diced

1½ cups fresh corn kernels (from about 2 ears)

1 cup fresh or frozen baby lima beans

½ teaspoon sugar

¼ teaspoon cayenne pepper

Remove the visible fat and the skin from the chicken thighs. Leave the thighbones in place, as they will help impart a rich flavor.

Cut the rabbit into four large sections. Place the chicken thighs and rabbit pieces on a baking sheet and season all sides with the salt and pepper.

Heat a large, heavy soup pot or Dutch oven over medium heat. Add the bacon and 2 tablespoons of the butter to the pot and begin to cook. Once the bacon is lightly browned, add the rabbit and chicken and brown on all sides. As the pieces are browned, transfer them to a platter.

In the same pot, cook the onion in the bacon drippings over medium heat until translucent, 3 to 5 minutes. Add the tomatoes, bay leaves, thyme, and Chicken Stock and bring to a simmer. While the liquid is heating, loosen and stir the brown drippings that may be stuck to the bottom of the pot. These morsels will add a lot of flavor to the stew.

Add the rabbit, chicken, and potatoes to the pot and simmer for 40 minutes, until the potatoes begin to fall apart. Then remove the chicken and rabbit and let cool while the liquid continues to simmer. Remove and discard the chicken and rabbit bones, then shred the meat by hand into smaller pieces. Return the meat to the pot and simmer for another 40 minutes. As the stew continues to cook, the potatoes will gradually thicken the liquid.

Add the corn and lima beans and season with the sugar and cayenne. Simmer for another 10 minutes to blend the flavors. Just prior to serving, remove the bay leaves and thyme and stir in the remaining 2 tablespoons butter.

"SMOKING HOT"
OXTAIL PEPPER POT

�֎

CULINARY COUSINS

SERVES
4 to **6**

ACTIVE TIME
45 MINS

🕐

TOTAL TIME
**5 HRS
45 MINS**

THIS GUYANESE CLASSIC IS traditionally eaten on Christmas Day. Cassareep, an essential ingredient, is a molasses-like syrup made from cassava root juice. It not only gives the pepper pot its characteristic taste but also acts as a preservative, allowing the stew to cook slowly for weeks if not months. Some pepper pots are reputed to have spent decades developing flavor on the back of a stove. Pepper pot was also popular in nineteenth-century Philadelphia, where it was called Philadelphia gumbo and sold on the city streets by women of West Indian origin.

CHEF'S NOTE

Cassareep and wiri wiri peppers, which are cherry-like in appearance, can be found in Caribbean markets or online. You may need to preorder oxtails and calf's feet from your local butcher.

2½ pounds oxtails (thick wide part from base of tail; ask your butcher to cut into 2½- to 3-inch sections)

1½ pounds boneless beef chuck, cut into 2-inch cubes

2 tablespoons kosher salt

1½ teaspoons freshly ground black pepper

½ cup packed light brown sugar, divided

1 cup cassareep, divided

3 tablespoons vegetable oil

1 cup yellow onion, finely chopped

8 garlic cloves, finely chopped

2½ pounds calf's feet (ask your butcher to cut into 2-inch sections)

6 cinnamon sticks

2 teaspoons whole cloves

3 wiri wiri peppers, or 2 Scotch bonnet or habanero peppers

5 to 6 cups cold water, plus more if needed

4 fresh thyme sprigs

3 bay leaves

Steamed white rice, for serving

Spread the oxtails and chuck on a baking sheet. Season the meat on all sides with the salt, pepper, ¼ cup of the brown sugar, and ¼ cup of the cassareep. Mix well and marinate at room temperature for 1 to 2 hours.

In a large stockpot, heat the vegetable oil over medium heat. Add the chuck and brown well on all sides. Transfer the browned pieces to a plate. Add the oxtails and brown well on all sides. Transfer the oxtails to a separate plate.

Add the onion and garlic to the stockpot and cook over medium heat until translucent, about 5 minutes. Add the browned oxtails, calf's feet, cinnamon sticks, cloves, and wiri wiri peppers to the pot. Add the water just to cover. Bring to a full boil and cook for 5 minutes, skimming off excess fat and froth. Reduce to a simmer, add 6 tablespoons of the remaining cassareep, and cook (skimming regularly) for about 1½ hours.

At this point the oxtails should be partially tender. Add the browned chuck, the remaining 6 tablespoons cassareep, thyme, and bay leaves and cook for another 1½ hours. During the cooking process, the water will reduce and the cassareep will thicken to a rich consistency. If at any point the stew is looking dry, add just enough additional water to keep it moist (½ cup at a time).

Once all the meat is tender and beginning to fall from the bones, carefully remove the meat and transfer to a serving platter. Cover with plastic wrap and keep warm. Remove the peppers and make two small incisions in them to release more heat, then return the peppers to the pot along with the remaining ¼ cup of brown sugar. Stir and briefly reduce to a rich sauce consistency, adjusting the seasoning with salt and pepper if needed.

Generously ladle the sauce over the oxtails and meat. Serve with rice.

PEANUTS

Peanuts were long thought to have originated on the African continent; they did not. They arrived there early on from South America through European trade, largely replacing the native Bambara groundnut, a similar legume. They returned to the northern part of the hemisphere with the slave trade, were fed to enslaved Africans on the Middle Passage, and, because of their triangular journey, were mistakenly believed by Americans to have been native to Africa. The terms *goober* or *goober peas*, from the Lingala *nguba*, point to the strength of the perceived African connection.

Peanut soups and dishes using ground peanuts abound on the western part of the African continent. In the United States and throughout the Americas, enslaved Africans and their descendants continued to use peanuts, especially in soups and confections. A peanut soup appears in one of the country's earliest cookbooks, and peanut patties have found their way into more than one school lunch box.

George Washington Carver, who oversaw the agricultural department at Tuskegee Institute, is best known for his peanut research. He did not, as many believe, invent peanut butter, but he did come up with more than three hundred uses for the legume, including more than one hundred ways to prepare it as food. Anyone who has ever sung "Goober Peas" at a Scout campfire has unknowingly acknowledged the journey of this most versatile legume from South America to Africa and back to the Americas.

Above: A man selling roasted peanuts in Washington, DC, 1972–75. Photograph by Milton Williams.

Left: Postcard of a praline seller in New Orleans, Louisiana, ca. 1910.

PRALINE SELLER, NEW ORLEANS, LA.

CLASSIC PEANUT BRITTLE

SENEGALESE
PEANUT SOUP

SERVES

4 to **6**

ACTIVE TIME
40 MINS
🕐
TOTAL TIME
1 HR

VEGETARIAN

THIS SOUP, BASED ON A popular peanut stew called *mafé*, probably gets its name from the fact that Senegal was the hub of the international peanut trade during the colonial period. During the last half of the nineteenth century, the French taxed Senegalese farmers, whose only means of paying was to grow peanuts, for which they received cash. All farmers were therefore encouraged to use part of their land to grow peanuts. Veritable mountains of peanuts were being shipped from West Africa to France for processing into soap, wax, and fodder. This rich curry-scented soup is a reminder of that trade in a soup bowl.

2 tablespoons peanut oil

1 cup yellow onion, finely chopped

1 tablespoon peeled fresh ginger, finely grated

2 garlic cloves, finely chopped

1 cup coarsely chopped skinless raw peanuts, plus 2 tablespoons chopped, for garnish

1 tablespoon curry powder

1 tablespoon tomato paste

1 jalapeño pepper, seeded and finely minced

6 cups Vegetable Stock (page 201)

2 sweet potatoes, peeled and diced

½ cup crushed tomatoes

1½ teaspoons kosher salt

2 bay leaves

¾ cup coconut milk

⅓ cup organic creamy peanut butter

Freshly ground black pepper

½ cup fresh cilantro leaves, for garnish

Pour the peanut oil into a large soup pot and heat over medium-low heat. Then add the onion, ginger, and garlic and cook until translucent, about 5 minutes. Add the peanuts and cook for another 3 minutes.

Add the curry powder, tomato paste, and jalapeño and cook over medium-low heat, stirring constantly, unitil the tomato paste has lightly caramelized, 3 to 4 minutes.

Now add the Vegetable Stock, sweet potatoes, crushed tomatoes, salt, and bay leaves and simmer uncovered for 20 minutes, until the potatoes are tender.

Remove 1½ cups of the soup (making sure to include broth, sweet potatoes, and other vegetables) and process in a blender until smooth. Return the pureed soup to the pot and bring to a simmer.

Add the coconut milk and cook for 5 minutes. Reduce the heat to the lowest setting and stir in the peanut butter until fully incorporated. Adjust the seasoning with salt and pepper to taste.

Just before serving, garnish with the cilantro leaves and chopped peanuts.

MAINS

BLACK-EYED PEA, GOLDEN CORN & CHANTERELLE EMPANADAS

MARYLAND CRAB CAKES

Top left: *Mr. Moore's Bar-b-que, 125th Street*, 1976; printed 2005. From the series *Harlem, USA*. Photograph by Dawoud Bey.

Right: *Leah Stirring, Red Coat (Sketch)*, 2010. Created by Gustave Blanche III.

Opposite, top: Patti LaBelle and two men holding crabs in Washington, DC, 1978. Photograph by Milton Williams.

Opposite, bottom: Flyer advertising Sneed's Restaurant in Baltimore, Maryland, 1940s.

MAINS

Feature: Agricultural South / 76

Thomas Downing's NYC Oyster Pan Roast / 79

Maryland Crab Cakes / 81

Shrimp & Grits / 82

Feature: Oysters / 84

Catfish Po'boy / 85

Whole Grilled Snapper with Creole Sauce / 86

Codfish Cakes / 87

Pan-Roasted Rainbow Trout / 88

Salmon Croquettes / 90

Fried Croaker with Sweet Onion
& Corn Hush Puppies / 93

Smothered Turkey Grillades
with Fried Apples / 94

Vietnamese Spiced Chicken Wings / 96

Chicken Livers & Grits with
Ham & Tomato Gravy / 99

Jamaican Jerk Chicken / 101

Buttermilk Fried Chicken / 103

Hot Fried Chicken & Waffles / 105

Feature: Barbecue / 107

Hickory-Smoked Barbecued Chicken / 109

Barbecued Beef Brisket Sandwich / 110

Hickory-Smoked Pork Shoulder / 112

Bacon-Wrapped Pan-Roasted Pork Chops / 114

Sticky Pork Ribs / 116

Curried Goat / 119

Limpin' Susan / 120

Trini Doubles / 121

Black-Eyed Pea, Golden Corn,
& Chanterelle Empanadas / 122

AGRICULTURAL SOUTH

This is the classic South of fried chicken and collard greens, corn bread, butter beans, and chopped barbecue sandwiches. But this is also the main region of enslavement and share-cropping, where deprivation and hardscrabble living led people to create well-seasoned meals out of ingenuity and scraps from others' tables. Although all African American food did not originate in the Agricultural South, this area holds a special place at the African American table.

It is the region where African Americans first attained respect as the chefs of the Founding Fathers, among them Hercules, George Washington's enslaved chef, and James Hemings, whose skills were so prized by Thomas Jefferson that Hemings was taken to France for further instruction.

It is equally the region that has been culinarily stereotyped by the figures of Aunt Jemima, Uncle Ben, and Rastus. All three entities were created by national brands using either actual African Americans or invented characters exemplifying real or imagined African American culinary excellence to their own end.

Here, enslaved farmers grew crops such as okra and black-eyed peas that connected them to their African origins. When allowed, they sold their harvests at venues such as the slave-run Sunday morning market in Alexandria, Virginia.

In the late 1800s, Gordonsville, Virginia, became the "Fried Chicken Capital of the World," thanks to its confluence of railroad lines and trade avenues and to a group of inventive African American women who seized a business opportunity and began bringing fried chicken to sell to the passengers on the trains. They called themselves waiter carriers and created personal wealth from the chicken and other items they sold in the days before dining-car train travel.

The Agricultural South was also home to George Washington Carver, whose work at Tuskegee Institute with sweet potatoes, peanuts, black-eyed peas, and more created agricultural benchmarks that still resonate today.

It is only fitting that twentieth-century culinary icon "Miss Edna" Lewis came from Freetown, Virginia, because her emphasis on fresh, local, seasonal foods was inextricably entwined with the rural love of land and what it can produce. Her achievements as both a chef and an author played a large part in putting the classic flavors of the Agricultural South on the national map.

Finally, it was at a lunch counter in Greensboro, North Carolina, on February 1, 1960, that one of the first civil rights sit-ins occurred. Within a few days, hundreds of protesters had joined the four young men who had initiated it, paralyzing the lunch counter and other local businesses. In less than two months, the movement had spread to more than a dozen states—a courageous wave of action that bound together food and the battle for civil rights as African Americans struggled to find a literal and metaphorical place at the American table.

BUTTERMILK FRIED CHICKEN

Opposite, top: Biscuits, the test of a true Southern baker, 2000.

Right: A family at picnic table in Greenville, Mississippi, 1950s–1960s. Photograph by Rev. Henry Clay Anderson.

THOMAS DOWNING'S

NYC OYSTER PAN ROAST

NORTHERN STATES

SERVES

6

ACTIVE TIME
40 MINS

TOTAL TIME
1 HR

IN NINETEENTH-CENTURY America, New York was the country's oyster-eating capital, but the bivalves were consumed with gusto in most coastal cities by all segments of the population and sold everywhere from street stalls to oyster refectories. African Americans were among the legendary oystermen and none was more famous than Thomas Downing, who made a fortune using his knowledge of oyster culture, ending up as one of the city's best-known restaurateurs. Unbeknownst to his fancy clients dining upstairs, the premises was a stop on the Underground Railroad.

CHEF'S NOTE

The Café uses Blue Point oysters because their large size makes a more generous portion in a pan roast. If they are not available, such northern oysters as Narragansetts or Pemaquids are excellent alternatives.

36 fresh oysters, preferably Blue Point

3½ tablespoons unsalted butter, at room temperature, divided

1 shallot, finely diced

⅓ cup white wine, preferably Chablis

3 tablespoons chili sauce

1 teaspoon Worcestershire sauce

1 cup heavy cream

12 baguette slices, cut ½ inch thick

¼ teaspoon Tabasco sauce

Shuck the oysters, being careful to reserve the liquor. Put the oysters in a medium bowl. Strain the liquor through a fine-mesh strainer into a cup measure. You should have about 1 cup liquor.

Preheat the oven to 375°F.

In a stainless steel saucepan, heat 1 tablespoon of the butter over gentle heat. Add the shallot and cook until tender and translucent, about 2 to 3 minutes, being careful not to let it brown. Then add the white wine and simmer until the liquid has reduced by half.

Once the wine is reduced, add the cup of oyster liquor, return to a simmer, and cook for an additional minute. Next add the chili sauce, Worcestershire sauce, and cream and simmer for an additional 2 minutes, until the volume is again reduced by half.

While the cream mixture is cooking, begin to make the baguette crisps. Using 1½ tablespoons of the butter, brush the baguette slices on both sides, arrange on a baking sheet, and toast in the oven until golden brown, about 3 minutes.

After the cream has reduced and slightly thickened, add the oysters. Over a gentle simmer, poach them for no longer than 2 minutes, taking care not to overcook them. They should appear slightly ruffled and lightly plumped.

Season the pan roast with the Tabasco sauce and the remaining 1 tablespoon butter. Mix well until fully incorporated. Divide the oysters evenly among individual bowls, ladle the chili cream over them, and serve with baguette toasts.

MARYLAND
CRAB CAKES

AGRICULTURAL
SOUTH

MAKES

12

CAKES

ACTIVE TIME
40 MINS

TOTAL TIME
**1 HR
45 MINS**

THE MARYLAND CRAB CAKE is a version of a fish cake that is particular to the Chesapeake area. Baltimore boasts two different types, both made from Maryland blue crab. One is lightly breaded, deep-fried, and may have a filler of some sort, and is often served with saltine crackers or on a hamburger bun. The version served at the Café is prepared from all lump crabmeat and is sautéed in butter.

CHEF'S NOTE

True Blue crabs are certified Maryland crabs harvested in the waters of the Chesapeake. If True Blue crabmeat is not available, substitute Gulf crabmeat to avoid frozen, pasteurized, or imported crabmeat. These cakes can also be made smaller for serving as party hors d'oeuvres.

2 pounds jumbo lump crabmeat, preferably True Blue certified crab

2 large egg yolks

1½ tablespoons mayonnaise, homemade or Duke's

2 teaspoons Dijon mustard

1 tablespoon Old Bay seasoning

2 teaspoons freshly squeezed lemon juice

1 dash Tabasco sauce

1 dash Worcestershire sauce

½ teaspoon sea salt

½ teaspoon cayenne pepper

1½ cups plain bread crumbs

½ cup vegetable oil

2 tablespoons unsalted butter

Lemon wedges, for serving

Pick through the crabmeat to remove any bits of shell. Be careful not to break up the lumps of crab too much. Place the meat in a large bowl and set aside.

In a small bowl, combine the egg yolks, mayonnaise, mustard, Old Bay seasoning, lemon juice, Tabasco sauce, Worcestershire sauce, salt, and cayenne, whisking until well blended. Spoon the mixture over the crabmeat and gently blend until the meat is coated, being careful not to break it up too much. Gently form the crab mixture into 12 three-ounce puck-shaped cakes.

Spread out the bread crumbs on a large plate. Lightly coat the crab cakes with the crumbs. Transfer the cakes to a platter and cover with plastic wrap. Chill the crab cakes in the refrigerator for at least 1 hour before cooking.

In a large nonstick skillet, heat the oil and butter over medium heat. When hot, working in batches to avoid crowding, add the crab cakes to the pan and cook, turning once, until golden brown, about 4 minutes on each side. Serve hot with lemon wedges.

SERVES

6

ACTIVE TIME
**1 HR
30 MINS**

🕐

TOTAL TIME
1 DAY

PLUS
OVERNIGHT
SOAKING
OF
THE GRITS

SHRIMP & GRITS

❈

THE SHRIMP VENDOR WAS a familiar sight on the streets of Charleston in the early twentieth century. One of the dishes that cooks might have prepared with their purchase is shrimp and grits, a Low Country natural that combined the abundant local shrimp with grits, a southern staple. For authenticity, use stone-ground grits; quick-cooking grits will not do.

CHEF'S NOTE

If they are available, buy shell-on local shrimp for the best flavor. Peeling and deveining them is a messy job, but if the fishmonger won't do it, you must.

GRITS

2½ cups artisanal stone-ground grits (coarse ground, yellow or white)

8 cups cold water

1 teaspoon kosher salt

½ cup half-and-half

2 tablespoons unsalted butter

SHRIMP

30 U15 Gulf shrimp (about 2 pounds), peeled and deveined

1 teaspoon sea salt

Freshly ground black pepper

1 tablespoon olive oil

3 ounces tasso ham or high-quality thick-sliced bacon, finely diced

2 leeks, white part only, well washed and cut into ½-inch-thick rounds

3 large tomatoes, peeled, seeded, and diced

3 tablespoons butter, cut into small pieces

1 pinch cayenne pepper

2 tablespoon fresh chives, finely snipped, for garnish

TO MAKE THE GRITS

THE NIGHT BEFORE

Pour the grits into a large bowl and cover with the water. Briefly stir, then allow to rest for about 10 minutes. During this time some corn hulls might rise to the top; if so, skim them off using a slotted spoon. Transfer the grits to the refrigerator and allow them to soak overnight.

THE NEXT DAY

Transfer the grits and water to a pot large enough to accommodate the expansion of the grits during cooking. Add the salt and place over high heat, stirring continuously until the grits reach a boil. Then reduce the heat to the lowest setting and gently cook, covered, for 1 hour. Stir every 9 or 10 minutes to prevent scorching.

After an hour of cooking, the grits should be done. Taste them to determine whether they are cooked; they should be creamy and tender to the tooth.

In a small saucepan, bring the half-and-half to a quick boil and immediately remove it from the heat. Finish the grits with the butter and half-and-half. Taste and adjust the seasoning with salt if needed.

TO MAKE THE SHRIMP

Preheat a large nonstick sauté pan over medium heat.

While the pan heats, season the shrimp on both sides with the salt and pepper. Set aside.

MAINS

Add the olive oil and ham to the hot pan and cook the ham until well browned and lightly crispy, about 3 to 4 minutes. Remove with a slotted spoon and transfer to a dish. Set aside.

To the same pan, add the leeks and quickly sauté over medium heat until golden and caramelized, about 4 minutes. Remove with a slotted spoon and transfer to a separate dish. Set aside.

Increase the heat to high, add the shrimp and crispy ham, and cook the shrimp on one side for 1½ minutes. Then turn the shrimp over, add the leeks and tomatoes, and sauté for 2 minutes longer, until the shrimp are pink and their flesh is opaque.

Remove the pan from the heat. Add the butter to the pan and swirl until the butter incorporates with the pan juices to form a sauce. Adjust the seasoning with salt, pepper, and cayenne.

TO SERVE THE SHRIMP AND GRITS

Portion out the grits into individual bowls and plates. Divide the shrimp and place on top of the grits. Spoon an equal amount of the leeks, tomatoes, ham, and sauce over each serving. Granish with the chives.

OYSTERS

The name "oyster" is given to a number of saltwater mollusks that grow in multiple coastal habitats around the country. Plentiful in the early nineteenth century, oysters were a truly democratic food, consumed with gusto by all segments of society. The black oystermen of the Middle Atlantic and the North generated considerable wealth by using their knowledge of oysters as a building block of entrepreneurship. By 1810, sixteen of the twenty-seven oystermen listed in the New York City directory were people of color.

No oysterman was more famous than Thomas Downing, the son of free people of color from the Virginia shore. He arrived in New York in 1819, realized that his understanding of oyster culture was a salable talent, established his own oyster beds, and built a business that at its height included one of the city's most elegant establishments, serving notables such as Charles Dickens and the Earl of Carlisle.

Although most oystermen were not as financially successful as Downing, they were all inventive and creative. In New Orleans, oyster shuckers learned early on that a gift of gab would earn larger tips, and they would talk, or "jive," with their patrons while working, giving rise to the phrase *shuckin' and jivin'* that lives on today.

Top: *Ed Atkins walking along the oyster beds*, Saint Helena Island, SC. Photograph by Pete Marovich.

Bottom: Oyster cans used by Maryland oyster-packing companies, late twentieth century.

CATFISH

PO'BOY

CREOLE COAST

SERVES
6

ACTIVE TIME
45 MINS

TOTAL TIME
1 HR

A NEW ORLEANS VARIATION on the hero sandwich, a po'boy can be prepared with meat (usually roast beef), hot sausage, fried chicken, or seafood of some sort and is traditionally served on Leidenheimer bread, a crusty, soft French-style loaf. Fried seafood versions often come "dressed" with lettuce, tomato, pickles, and mayonnaise. The origin of the name "po'boy" is hotly debated. The sandwich was already on the scene in the late 1800s, but in those days it was known as an oyster loaf. Some historians believe the term *po'boy* originated during the city's 1929 streetcar strike, when the sandwiches were eaten by the "poor boys" on the picket lines. Whatever the origin of the term, these sandwiches are a New Orleans staple, and the best can be sampled at the annual Oak Street Po-Boy Festival held in November.

RED PEPPER REMOULADE

- 1 cup mayonnaise, preferably Duke's
- ¼ cup Dijon mustard
- 1 tablespoon cider vinegar
- 1½ tablespoons prepared horseradish
- 1 shallot, finely diced
- ¼ cup roasted red pepper, chopped into a paste
- 1 teaspoon freshly squeezed lemon juice
- 1 teaspoon Tabasco sauce
- ½ teaspoon smoked paprika
- ½ teaspoon kosher salt
- 1 tablespoon fresh flat-leaf parsley, chopped

PO'BOYS

- 6 catfish fillets (about 5 ounces each)
- 3 tablespoons Creole Spice Blend (page 196)
- 1 large egg
- 1½ cups buttermilk, preferably full fat
- ½ cup all-purpose flour
- 1½ cups cornmeal, preferably stone-ground
- ½ teaspoon kosher salt
- 1 cup peanut or vegetable oil, for frying
- 6 (6-inch) hoagie rolls, split
- 2 tablespoons unsalted butter, at room temperature
- 1 cup romaine lettuce, shredded
- 12 slices vine-ripened tomato

TO MAKE THE RED PEPPER REMOULADE

Combine all the remoulade ingredients in a medium bowl, whisking until well blended. Cover and chill. It will keep for up to 3 days.

TO MAKE THE PO'BOYS

Season the catfish fillets on both sides with the Creole Spice Blend. Set aside to marinate for 15 minutes.

In a small bowl, whisk together the egg and buttermilk until blended. In a pie plate, mix together the flour, cornmeal, and salt. Dip each catfish fillet into the buttermilk wash to coat well on both sides, draining off the excess. Dredge the fillets in the cornmeal mix to coat both sides, then lay on a wire rack set over a baking sheet while the oil heats.

Pour the oil into a large cast iron skillet and heat over medium-high heat. Working in batches if needed to avoid crowding, fry the catfish for about 3 minutes on each side, or until golden brown and the flesh is opaque and flakes. Using a slotted spatula, transfer the fillets to a platter lined with paper towels. Pour out the oil, wipe the pan clean, and place over low heat.

Brush the cut sides of the rolls with the butter. Place the rolls, cut side down, in the skillet until lightly toasted. On each roll, layer 1 fried fillet, some lettuce, 2 tomato slices, and a dollop of Red Pepper Remoulade.

SERVES

4 to 6

ACTIVE TIME
30 MINS

TOTAL TIME
1 HR

WHOLE
GRILLED SNAPPER
WITH CREOLE SAUCE

THE TERM *CREOLE* IS USUALLY applied when foods are accompanied with a tomato sauce rich with the Creole culinary holy trinity of bell pepper, onion, and celery. Variations on the sauce appear in New Orleans, the Bahamas, and in the Caribbean. Here, it accompanies a red snapper that is grilled whole.

CHEF'S NOTE

This snapper cooked on the bone is especially well suited to family-style dining. The fish can also be roasted in a 400°F oven for 15 minutes.

1 (5-pound) red snapper, scaled, gutted, and gills removed

4 tablespoons unsalted butter, divided

1 tablespoon olive oil, plus more for brushing the fish

⅓ cup yellow onion, finely chopped

2 garlic cloves, finely chopped

¾ cup green bell pepper, finely diced

½ cup scallions, white and green parts, sliced

⅔ cup celery, finely diced

½ teaspoon smoked paprika

1 tablespoon tomato paste

1 tablespoon all-purpose flour

1¾ cups Chicken Stock (page 200)

1 (16-ounce) can crushed tomatoes

3 bay leaves

3 fresh thyme sprigs

2 teaspoons Creole Spice Blend (page 196)

2 or 3 dashes Worcestershire sauce

1 or 2 dashes hot sauce

1 teaspoon kosher salt, plus more for seasoning fish

Freshly ground black pepper

Carolina Gold Rice Pilaf (page 48) for serving

Rinse the fish under cold water. Pat it dry inside and out with a paper towel and transfer to a baking sheet. With a sharp knife, make four evenly spaced fine incisions into the skin of the fish on both sides (do not cut into the flesh). Refrigerate the fish while preparing the sauce.

In a large saucepan, heat 1 tablespoon of the butter and the oil over medium heat. Add the onion and garlic and cook until translucent, about 5 minutes. Add the bell pepper, scallions, and celery and cook for 4 minutes, stirring occasionally. Then add the paprika and tomato paste and cook, stirring, for 3 minutes. Add in the flour and cook, stirring, for 3 minutes.

Add the Chicken Stock, crushed tomatoes, bay leaves, and thyme and bring to a simmer. Add the Creole Spice Blend, Worcestershire sauce, hot sauce, salt, and pepper to taste. Cook for 30 more minutes.

While the sauce is cooking, prepare a medium fire in a charcoal or gas grill. Generously season the fish on both sides as well as inside the cavity with salt and pepper. Brush the skin on both sides with a light coating of olive oil.

Place the fish on the grill and close the cover. Grill for 7 minutes. Using two large grill spatulas and taking care not to break its skin, carefully turn the fish over and cook for another 7 to 8 minutes, until the flesh is opaque and flakes. Transfer the fish to a large serving platter.

Just prior to serving, whisk the remaining 3 tablespoons butter into the sauce and adjust the seasoning if needed. Generously ladle the sauce over the fish, reserving sauce for the table. Serve with Carolina Gold Rice Pilaf.

CODFISH CAKES

NORTHERN
STATES

MAKES
10
C AKES

ACTIVE TIME
45 MINS

TOTAL TIME
**1 HR
45 MINS**

THE COD FISH CAKE IS TO New England what the crab cake is to Maryland (page 81). In the past, both were prepared from fresh local seafood that was abundant enough to be inexpensive. Like crab cakes, these cakes can also be made smaller and served as hors d'oeuvres. Both sizes can be accompanied with *gribiche* sauce, a lighter, tastier French version of tartar sauce using cornichons, capers, and hard-boiled egg. If fresh chervil isn't available, fresh flat-leaf parsley makes a good substitute.

CHEF'S NOTE

In Baltimore, cooks make similar codfish cakes bound with mashed potatoes instead of bread crumbs, sandwich them between saltines, dress them with yellow mustard, and call them "coddies."

COD

1½ cups cold water

½ lemon, sliced

½ teaspoon black peppercorns

½ teaspoon sea salt

2 bay leaves

6 parsley stems

1 shallot, thinly sliced

1 pound cod fillets

CODFISH CAKES

1 tablespoon butter

2 shallots, minced

1 celery stalk, finely diced

1 garlic clove, finely chopped

2 tablespoons mayonnaise, preferably Duke's

1 teaspoon whole-grain mustard

1 teaspoon Dijon mustard

½ teaspoon lemon zest, finely grated

2 teaspoons Old Bay seasoning

½ teaspoon smoked paprika

¼ cup fresh chives, finely snipped

⅓ bunch fresh flat-leaf parsley, chopped

1 teaspoon sea salt

½ teaspoon freshly ground black pepper

2 large eggs, beaten

1½ cups plain dried bread crumbs, divided

½ cup vegetable oil

Lemon wedges, for serving

Gribiche Sauce (page 202), for serving

TO POACH THE COD

In a medium saucepan, combine all the ingredients except the cod, bring to a gentle simmer, and simmer for 3 minutes. Add the cod and simmer gently for 7 minutes, until the flesh is opaque and flakes. Using a slotted spatula, transfer the cod to a plate, let cool, and then chill well, 25 to 30 minutes.

TO MAKE THE COD CAKES

In a small sauté pan, melt the butter over medium heat. Add the shallots, celery, and garlic and cook until translucent, about 5 minutes. Transfer to a large bowl and let cool, then add the mayonnaise, both mustards, lemon zest, Old Bay, paprika, chives, parsley, salt, pepper, eggs, and ½ cup of the bread crumbs and mix well.

Flake the chilled cod into the mayonnaise mixture and stir gently to mix well. Form the fish mixture into 10 uniform patties, coat the patties on all sides with the remaining 1 cup bread crumbs, and place on a baking sheet. Refrigerate for 30 minutes.

In a large skillet, heat the oil over medium heat. Working in batches to avoid crowding, fry the cakes, turning once, until a golden crust forms, 3 to 4 minutes on each side. Serve hot with the lemon wedges and Gribiche Sauce.

ACTIVE TIME
1 HR

🕐 TOTAL TIME
**1 HR
50 MINS**

PAN-ROASTED
RAINBOW TROUT

THIS MUSTARD GREENS-stuffed rainbow trout makes an impressive main course when presented on a large platter and dressed with hazelnut brown butter sauce. Rice is the perfect accompaniment, as it will soak up any of the excess nutty butter.

4 tablespoons olive oil, divided, plus more for the baking sheet

1 large Vidalia or other sweet onion, thinly sliced

2 garlic cloves, chopped into a fine paste

1 pound mustard greens, stemmed, washed, and roughly chopped

1 cup oil-packed sun-dried tomatoes, drained and chopped

2 cups Corn Bread Croutons (see Baby Kale Salad, page 25)

½ teaspoon kosher salt, plus more for serving

Freshly ground black pepper

6 (12-ounce) whole trout
(ask the fishmonger to prepare the fish as whole, headless, butterflied, and boned)

HAZELNUT BROWN BUTTER SAUCE

8 tablespoons (1 stick) butter

½ cup blanched hazelnuts, coarsely chopped

Juice of 1 lemon

¼ cup chopped fresh sage leaves

½ teaspoon kosher salt

Freshly ground black pepper

Heat a large skillet over medium heat. Pour in 2 tablespoons of the olive oil and add the onion. Reduce the temperature to low and slowly caramelize the onion, cooking for 15 to 18 minutes. Add the garlic paste and cook for another 2 minutes.

Add the mustard greens and cook until the greens have wilted. Increase the heat to medium, stir in the tomatoes, and cook for 3 to 5 minutes, until the moisture has evaporated. Remove from the heat and transfer the mixture to a medium bowl.

Fold the croutons into the mustard green mixture and season with the salt and pepper to taste. Cover and chill in the refrigerator for at least 30 minutes.

Place the trout on a baking sheet, unfolding one side of each fish to open it like a book. Lightly season with salt and pepper. Now spoon about 3 tablespoons of the corn bread stuffing into each cavity. Make sure each fish has an even balance of corn bread, greens, tomatoes, and onion. Gently spread the stuffing the full length of the trout fillets; the depth of the stuffing should be about ½ inch. Fold the top half of the fish back over the stuffing. Transfer to the refrigerator to chill for 20 minutes. Preheat the oven to 200°F.

Add the remaining 2 tablespoons olive oil to a large nonstick skillet set over high heat. When the oil is hot, add 3 trout and cook for 4 minutes on one side, then carefully flip the fish over and cook the second side for another 4 minutes, until a golden brown crust has formed and the flesh flakes and is opaque. Transfer the fish to a clean, lightly oiled baking sheet and place in the warm oven while the remaining fish cook. Repeat with the trout in 3 more batches, keeping them warm in the oven.

To make the Hazelnut Brown Butter Sauce, pour off the oil from the skillet and return the pan to the stovetop. Add the butter and heat until it is a light golden color, about 2 minutes. Add the hazelnuts and cook until the butter develops a rich golden color, 1 to 2 minutes more. Remove the skillet from the heat and stir in the lemon juice and sage. Season with the salt and pepper to taste.

Transfer the trout to the indivdual plates, spoon the Hazelnut Brown Butter Sauce over the top, and serve.

MAKES

6

CROQUETTES

ACTIVE TIME
40 MINS
🕐
TOTAL TIME
2 HRS

SALMON

CROQUETTES

CANNED SALMON IS OFTEN A
pantry staple in African American
households, and salmon croquettes
prepared from it have graced
many a dinner table when cooks
are too busy to shop. Canned
salmon also shows up on the
breakfast table, sometimes
scrambled into eggs and sometimes as croquettes accompanied
by grits.

CHEF'S NOTE

Because of their superior taste, the
Café uses freshly poached salmon
fillets for the croquettes in place
of the traditional canned salmon.
Be sure to remove any pin bones
before poaching the salmon fillet.

SALMON

1½ cups cold water

½ lemon, sliced

½ teaspoon black peppercorns

½ teaspoon sea salt

2 bay leaves

4 dill stems

1 shallot, thinly sliced

1 pound salmon fillet,
skin removed

CROQUETTES

1 tablespoon unsalted butter

1 celery stalk, finely diced

3 scallions, white and light green
parts, thinly sliced

1 garlic clove, finely chopped

2 tablespoons mayonnaise,
preferably Duke's

2 teaspoons Dijon mustard

1 teaspoon finely grated lemon zest

1½ teaspoons Old Bay seasoning

¼ cup minced fresh dill leaves

1 large egg yolk, beaten, plus
2 large eggs, divided

1 teaspoon sea salt

½ teaspoon freshly ground
black pepper

1 cup all-purpose flour

1 cup panko bread crumbs

½ cup vegetable oil

Lemon wedges, for serving

Gribiche Sauce (page opposite),
for serving

TO POACH THE SALMON

In a medium saucepan, combine the water, lemon, peppercorns, salt, bay
leaves, dill, and shallot, bring to a gentle simmer, and simmer for 3 minutes.
Add the salmon fillet and simmer gently over low heat for 7 minutes, until
the flesh flakes and is opaque. Using a slotted spatula, transfer the salmon
to a plate, let cool, and chill well, 25 to 30 minutes.

TO MAKE THE CROQUETTES

In a large sauté pan, melt the butter over medium heat. Add the celery,
scallions, and garlic and cook until translucent, about 5 minutes. Transfer
to a medium bowl and let cool.

Add the mayonnaise, mustard, lemon zest, Old Bay seasoning, dill, egg yolk,
salt, and pepper to the bowl and mix well.

Flake the chilled salmon into the mayonnaise mixture and stir gently to
mix well. Form the salmon mixture into six uniform cylinder-shaped pieces
(about 3 ounces each) and roll each piece in the flour, coating all sides. Place
the croquettes on a baking sheet.

Beat the 2 whole eggs in a small bowl. Put the bread crumbs in a separate small, shallow bowl.

Dip a croquette into the egg to fully coat, then gently remove from the bowl with a fork, draining off the excess egg. Now transfer the croquette to the bread crumbs, fully coat, and place back on the baking sheet. Repeat this process until all the croquettes have been coated. Refrigerate the croquettes for 30 minutes to allow them to firm.

In a large, heavy-bottomed skillet, heat the vegetable oil over medium heat. Add the croquettes and fry, turning as needed, for 5 to 6 minutes, until golden brown on all sides.

Serve hot with lemon wedges and Gribiche Sauce.

GRIBICHE SAUCE

1 cup mayonnaise, preferably Duke's
½ cup fresh chervil, chopped
¼ cup fresh chives, snipped
1 shallot, finely minced
2 hard-boiled eggs, finely chopped
6 cornichons, chopped
2 teaspoons capers, chopped
2 teaspoons Dijon mustard
¼ teaspoon cayenne pepper
Salt
Freshly ground black pepper

Combine the mayonnaise, chervil, chives, shallot, eggs, cornichons, capers, mustard, and cayenne in a medium mixing bowl, and whisk until well blended. Season with salt and pepper to taste.

CONTINENTAL
UNITED STATES

MAKES

1½ cups

ACTIVE TIME
10 MINS

TOTAL TIME
10 MINS

FRIED CROAKER
WITH SWEET ONION & CORN HUSH PUPPIES

CREOLE COAST

SERVES
4

ACTIVE TIME
30 MINS

TOTAL TIME
40 MINS

THE ATLANTIC CROAKER, a member of the drum family, is a popular choice for fish fries. It is usually found on the muddy and sandy bottoms of bays from Massachusetts to Mexico and is a frequent catch of recreational fishermen, especially in the Chesapeake area.

CHEF'S NOTE

Whole fish are the traditional way of serving this dish because the result is more flavorful than fillets.

1½ cups all-purpose flour

4 tablespoons Creole Spice Blend (page 196)

½ teaspoon kosher salt, plus more for seasoning fish

1 pinch cayenne pepper

4 (1-pound) croaker, porgy, spot, or other panfish, heads cut off, scaled, gutted, and gills removed

1½ cups vegetable oil, for frying

Lemon wedges, for serving

Sweet Onion & Corn Hush Puppies with Red Pepper Remoulade, for serving (page 146)

In a medium baking dish, mix the flour, Creole Spice Blend, salt, and cayenne until well blended.

With a few paper towels, dry the cavities of the fish. Pat the skin dry as well, and season the cavity and exterior of each fish with salt. Dredge the exterior of each fish in the seasoned flour to coat well.

Pour the vegetable oil into a large cast iron skillet and heat to 350°F on a deep-frying thermometer (or use a tabletop deep fryer).

Fry the fish in the hot oil turning once, until crisp, and the flesh flakes and is opaque, 4 to 5 minutes. Transfer to a platter lined with paper towels to drain off excess oil. Serve hot with lemon wedges, and the Sweet Onion & Corn Hush Puppies with Red Pepper Remoulade.

SERVES

4 to 6

ACTIVE TIME
50 MINS

🕐

TOTAL TIME
**1 HR
30 MINS**

SMOTHERED
TURKEY GRILLADES
WITH FRIED APPLES

A SOUTHERN LOUISIANA French term, grillades are medallions of meat smothered in a rich gravy. They are usually prepared from beef or veal and occasionally from pork. New Orleans Creoles often serve them over grits at breakfast or brunch.

CHEF'S NOTE

At the Café, grillades are prepared with turkey and served with Johnnycakes (page 149) and fried apples.

SAUCE

1½ teaspoons butter or bacon drippings

½ cup yellow onion, finely chopped

2 garlic cloves, finely chopped

¼ cup green bell pepper, finely diced

¼ cup celery, finely diced

1½ teaspoons Creole Spice Blend (page 196)

2 teaspoons all-purpose flour

2 cups Chicken Stock (page 200)

¼ cup fresh sage, chopped

1 teaspoon Worcestershire sauce

Salt

Freshly ground black pepper

FRIED APPLES

1 tablespoon butter

1 large Gala apple, peeled, cored, and cut into wedges (about 1 cup)

¼ teaspoon sugar

⅛ teaspoon ground cinnamon

TURKEY GRILLADES

2½ pounds boneless turkey breast, cut into thin slices and pounded to ¼ inch thick

1 teaspoon kosher salt

Freshly ground black pepper

¼ cup all-purpose flour

1 tablespoon butter

1 tablespoon canola oil

TO MAKE THE SAUCE

Melt the butter in a medium saucepan over medium-low heat. Add the onion and garlic and cook until lightly golden, 8 to 10 minutes.

Add the bell pepper and celery and cook for another 5 minutes. Then add the Creole Spice Blend and flour, stirring well to fully coat the vegetables.

Pour in the Chicken Stock and bring to a boil, then reduce the heat and gently simmer for 20 more minutes, until dark golden in color.

TO MAKE THE FRIED APPLES

Melt the butter in a medium skillet over medium heat. Add the apple wedges and sauté until lightly golden, about 6 to 8 minutes. Add the sugar and cinnamon and cook for another 3 minutes, until the apples are lightly caramelized but still firm.

TO MAKE THE TURKEY GRILLADES

Preheat the oven to 350°F.

Arrange the turkey breast slices on a work surface and season on both sides with the salt and pepper. Pour the flour into a medium, shallow bowl and dredge the turkey slices in the flour, coating evenly.

Melt the butter with canola oil in a large ovenproof skillet over a medium heat. Add the turkey and fry on both sides until a golden crust has formed. Drain off the excess fat. Add the sauce to the skillet and coat the turkey well. Transfer the skillet to the oven and bake for 20 minutes, until the turkey is cooked through.

When the grillades are cooked, finish the sauce with the sage and Worcestershire sauce and season to taste with salt and pepper. Spoon the sauce over the grillades and serve with the fried apples.

CAFÉ SPECIAL

SERVES
6 to **8**

ACTIVE TIME
45 MINS

TOTAL TIME
1 DAY
REFRIGERATE OVERNIGHT

VIETNAMESE SPICED
CHICKEN WINGS

CREATED FOR A SPECIAL promotion at the Café, these chicken wings have a decidedly Asian flavor. They owe their unique taste to a heady mix of five-spice powder, lime juice, sambal chilie paste, and the *nước mắm* fish sauce.

CHEF'S NOTE

These wings can also be cooked indoors or on a stove top grill pan.

3 pounds chicken wings, each split into two pieces

6 garlic cloves, chopped into a fine paste

¼ cup freshly squeezed lime juice

½ cup nước mắm fish sauce or other Vietnamese fish sauce

¼ cup soy sauce

¼ cup packed light brown sugar

2 tablespoons Creole mustard, such as Zatarain's

1 tablespoon five-spice powder

2 lemongrass stalks, white bulb-like sections only, cut into 1-inch slices

2 tablespoons vegetable oil

2 tablespoons sambal chile paste

3 Thai peppers, thinly sliced, for garnish

½ cup fresh cilantro leaves, for garnish

1 lime, thinly sliced, for garnish

THE NIGHT BEFORE

Put the chicken wings in a large bowl.

To make the marinade, combine the garlic, lime juice, fish sauce, soy sauce, sugar, mustard, five-spice powder, lemongrass, oil, and chile paste in a medium bowl and mix well. Pour the marinade over the chicken wings and mix until evenly coated. Cover tightly with plastic wrap and refrigerate overnight.

THE NEXT DAY

Preheat a medium fire in a charcoal or gas grill.

Drain off and reserve the marinade from the chicken wings. Place the wings on a baking sheet. Transfer the marinade to a saucepan and bring the mixture to a full boil. Reduce the heat to the lowest setting and keep the sauce warm.

Place the wings on the grill and cook them, basting frequently with the marinade. Move the wings around on the grill and turn them over regularly. They will become richly caramelized and lightly charred, but be sure to avoid burning. The wings will be cooked when they have reached an internal temperature of 165°F on an instant-read thermometer, about 18 minutes.

Transfer to a platter and garnish with the Thai peppers, cilantro, and lime.

CHICKEN LIVERS & GRITS
WITH HAM & TOMATO GRAVY

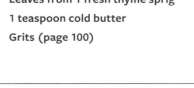

AGRICULTURAL
SOUTH

SERVES

6

ACTIVE TIME
15 MINS

⏱

TOTAL TIME
1 DAY
PLUS
OVERNIGHT
SOAKING OF
THE GRITS

DURING THE PERIOD OF slavery, the less noble parts (offal) of many animals, such as chicken livers, gizzards, and hearts, typically turned up on African American tables. Here, chicken livers are smothered in a rich brown sauce with a hint of tomato and then spooned over grits. They can also be served over rice or with the hot bread of your choice for sopping up the gravy.

CHEF'S NOTE

Wondra flour has an ultrafine texture and does not cake. It can be found in well-stocked supermarkets and online.

1 pound chicken livers, preferably all-natural or organic, trimmed of connective tissue

1 teaspoon kosher salt

Freshly ground black pepper

1 cup Wondra quick-mixing flour

1 tablespoon bacon drippings or canola oil

2 ounces cooked salt-cured country ham, diced

4 shallots, thinly sliced

1 large vine-ripened tomato, peeled, seeded, and diced

1 cup Brown Sauce (page 100)

Leaves from 1 fresh thyme sprig

1 teaspoon cold butter

Grits (page 100)

Wash the chicken livers in cold water, drain, and transfer to a plate lined with paper towels to absorb excess moisture. Season the chicken livers on both sides with salt and pepper. Lightly dust the livers with the Wondra flour, coating completely.

Heat the bacon drippings in a large skillet over medium-high heat. Add the chicken livers, country ham, and shallots. Sear the livers on one side for 2 minutes, then flip to the other side and cook for 2 minutes longer. Remove the livers and transfer them to a warm plate. The livers should be plump and rosy.

Now add the diced tomato to the pan and sauté over high heat for 1 minute. Stir in the Brown Sauce and thyme leaves and bring to a full boil, then reduce the heat and simmer for 1 minute. Return the livers to the pan, coating them well with the sauce. Quickly stir in the butter.

The livers should be served medium-rare, medium at most. Portion the grits into bowls and distribute the livers and gravy evenly.

continues

MAKES

3

CUPS

ACTIVE TIME
30 MINS

TOTAL TIME
**2 HRS
30 MINS**

1 tablespoon olive oil

1 cup shallots, chopped

½ cup leek, white and light green parts, chopped

¼ cup carrot, peeled and chopped

¼ cup celery, chopped

2 garlic cloves

1 tablespoon tomato paste

1 teaspoon sherry vinegar

1 cup red wine

2 fresh bay leaves

2 fresh thyme sprigs

½ teaspoon black peppercorns

6 cups Veal Stock (page 201) or low-sodium beef stock

BROWN SAUCE

Heat the olive oil in a medium saucepan over medium-high heat. Add the shallots and leeks and sauté until lightly caramelized, about 2 minutes. Add the carrot, celery, and garlic and cook for 3 more minutes. Stir in the tomato paste and cook for 3 minutes longer.

Add the sherry vinegar. With a wooden spoon, scrape up the bits from the bottom of the pan. Add the red wine, bay leaves, thyme sprigs, and peppercorns and gently boil the sauce until a syrupy consistency is achieved.

Add the Veal Stock and simmer very gently for 2 hours. Strain through a fine-mesh strainer and cool immediately. Refrigerate and use within 4 days, or freeze in 1-cup containers and use within 3 months.

MAKES

6

CUPS

ACTIVE TIME
10 MINS

TOTAL TIME
**1HR
10 MINS**
PLUS
OVERNIGHT
SOAKING OF
THE GRITS

2½ cups artisanal stone-ground grits (coarse ground yellow or white)

8 cups cold water

½ cup half-and-half

2 tablespoons butter

1 teaspoon kosher salt

GRITS

THE NIGHT BEFORE
Pour the grits into a large bowl and cover with the water. Briefly stir, then allow to rest for about 10 minutes. During this time some corn hulls might rise to the top; if so, skim them off using a slotted spoon. Transfer the grits to the refrigerator to soak overnight.

THE NEXT DAY
Transfer the grits and water to a pot large enough to accommodate the expansion of the grits during cooking. Place over high heat, stirring continuously until the grits reach a boil. Then reduce the heat to the lowest setting and gently cook, covered, for 1 hour. Stir every 9 or 10 minutes to prevent scorching.

After an hour of cooking, the grits should be done. Taste them to determine whether they are cooked; they should be creamy and tender.

In a small saucepan, bring the half-an-half to a quick boil and immediately remove it from the heat. Finish the grits with the butter and the half-and-half, and season with the salt. Serve immediately.

JERK CHICKEN

CULINARY
COUSINS

SERVES
6 to **8**

ACTIVE TIME
20 MINS
⊙
TOTAL TIME
1 DAY
REFRIGERATE
OVERNIGHT

SPICY, PEPPERY, ALLSPICE-scented jerk, Jamaica's entry into the barbecue sweepstakes, involves grilling and steaming over smoke from a fire of allspice wood, also known as pimento wood. The method evolved from the traditional war food of the Maroons, formerly enslaved Jamaicans who escaped, formed independent settlements, and fought against the British for their freedom in the mid-seventeenth century. Several Maroon communities remain to this day.

CHEF'S NOTE

Some of the best versions of jerk chicken on the island today can be found at Boston Beach, near Port Antonio. Get a more flavorful smoke by adding pimento wood chips or chunks (available online) to the grill fire. In the absence of pimento wood, soak a handful of allspice berries in water and throw them on top of the hot coals when grilling.

2 whole chickens, about 2½ pounds each, each bird cut into four pieces

3 cups Wet Jerk Rub (page 197)

Rice & Pigeon Peas (page 49), for serving

THE NIGHT BEFORE

Put the chicken pieces in a large bowl and cover with the Wet Jerk Rub, tossing well to ensure that all the pieces are fully coated. Transfer to an airtight container and refrigerate for at least 6 hours or up to overnight.

THE NEXT DAY

Prepare a medium-hot fire **in a charcoal grill** (charcoal will offer a richer flavor, but a gas grill can be used). If available, add pimento wood chips for extra flavor.

Place the chicken on the grill and close the lid. Cook for about 40 minutes; the meat is done when it reaches an internal temperature of 165°F on an instant-read thermometer.

Serve hot with Rice & Pigeon Peas.

BUTTERMILK
FRIED CHICKEN

SERVES

4 to 6

ACTIVE TIME
45 MINS

TOTAL TIME
1 DAY
REFRIGERATE
OVERNIGHT

THE HISTORY OF FRIED chicken is complex. Post-emancipation, it enabled African American women like the waiter carriers of Gordonsville, Virginia, to enjoy financial freedom (see page 76). Packed in shoeboxes, it traveled northward and westward with families in the Great Migration. Later, it became a popular offering in soul food restaurants.

CHEF'S NOTE

For the best flavor, use organic or all-natural free-range chicken. Peanut oil makes an excellent choice for frying and accents the flavor of the finished chicken. Corn or canola oil can be substituted. A cast iron skillet is traditional and conducts and transfers heat evenly, which makes for a crispier chicken.

4 pounds bone-in chicken pieces (halved split breasts, thighs, and/or drumsticks)

Poultry Brine (page 198)

1 quart buttermilk, preferably full fat

1 teaspoon kosher salt

½ teaspoon freshly ground black pepper

½ teaspoon sweet Hungarian paprika

4 to 6 dashes Tabasco sauce

2 garlic cloves, crushed (not chopped)

2 or 3 fresh thyme sprigs

3 cups peanut oil, for frying

Seasoned Flour (page 104)

Place the chicken pieces in a storage container or a large stainless steel bowl.

Pour the brine over the chicken pieces, ensuring that they are fully covered by the brine. Transfer to the refrigerator and let the chicken rest for 6 to 8 hours.

Remove the chicken from the refrigerator and drain off the brine. Be sure to discard the liquid.

To make the buttermilk "soak," combine the buttermilk, salt, pepper, paprika, Tabasco, garlic, and thyme in a large bowl. Add the drained chicken pieces and turn them to coat well. Refrigerate for 4 hours.

When you are ready to cook the chicken, heat a 10-inch cast iron skillet over medium heat. Add the oil and allow it to slowly heat to 350°F on a deep-frying thermometer.

While the oil is heating, drain the chicken in a colander. Put the Seasoned Flour in a medium shallow bowl. Dredge the chicken, one piece at a time, in the flour until coated on all sides. Transfer each piece to a wire rack set over a baking sheet, placing the pieces side by side but not touching. Confirm that the temperature of the frying oil is at 350°F and then add five or six pieces of the chicken, being careful not to crowd the pan. The oil should reach just to the top of the chicken and should always be at 350°F. Fry the chicken until deep golden brown all over and the internal temperature reaches 165°F on an instant-read thermometer, 20 to 25 minutes. Using a slotted spoon or tongs, transfer to a wire rack to drain. Repeat with the remaining chicken.

continues

MAKES

4

CUPS

ACTIVE TIME
8 MINS

🕐

TOTAL TIME
8 MINS

4 cups all-purpose flour

2 tablespoons kosher salt

1½ tablespoons onion powder

1 tablespoon freshly ground black pepper

1 tablespoon garlic powder

1½ teaspoons sweet Hungarian paprika

1 teaspoon freshly ground white pepper

SEASONED FLOUR

In a large mixing bowl, combine all the ingredients. Whisk the mixture until the seasonings are well blended with the flour.

If not using right away, transfer to an airtight container and store at room temperature for up to 1 month.

HOT FRIED
CHICKEN & WAFFLES

NORTHERN
STATES

SERVES
4 to **6**

ACTIVE TIME
45 MINS
🕐
TOTAL TIME
**6 HRS
45 MINS**

WHERE THE CLASSIC COMBI-nation of chicken and waffles originated is disputed, but most agree that Wells, an eatery in Harlem, was where it became best known. The spot was a late-night hangout for musicians, who, having finished their gigs around town, would head to Wells to wind down and savor a meal that combined the fried chicken of dinner with the waffles that meant breakfast.

CHEF'S NOTE

At the Café, southern ingredients like sorghum, cornmeal, and bourbon are added for a new twist on the traditional dish. Look for corn flour at well stocked super-markets and specialty food stores; Bob's Red Mill is a popular brand.

CHICKEN

6 (about 5 ounces each) boneless, skinless chicken breasts

2 cups buttermilk

3 garlic cloves, chopped

1 tablespoon fresh thyme leaves

2 teaspoons hot sauce

½ teaspoon smoked paprika

¼ teaspoon kosher salt

⅛ teaspoon freshly ground black pepper

1½ cups Seasoned Flour (page 104)

1½ cups peanut or vegetable oil

SPICED SORGHUM SYRUP

2 ounces bourbon

1 teaspoon pure vanilla extract, preferably Bourbon vanilla

2 cinnamon sticks

2 whole cloves

Zest of ½ orange (no white pith)

1½ cups sorghum syrup

WAFFLES

½ cup yellow cornmeal, preferably stone-ground

½ cup corn flour

1 cup all-purpose flour

2 teaspoons baking powder

½ teaspoon baking soda

½ teaspoon fine sea salt

3 large eggs, separated

1 cup buttermilk, preferably full fat

1 teaspoon freshly ground black pepper

2 tablespoons unsalted butter, melted

Salted butter, for serving

TO MAKE THE CHICKEN

Trim the chicken breasts of any fat or skin and pat dry with a paper towel.

Combine the buttermilk, garlic, thyme, hot sauce, paprika, salt, and pepper in a medium bowl and mix well.

Put the chicken in a large bowl and pour over the seasoned buttermilk. Marinate in the refrigerator for 4 to 6 hours. (Toward the end of the marinating time, prepare the waffle batter.)

When the marinating is complete, drain the chicken in a colander, then dredge each breast in Seasoned Flour, coating well on all sides.

Heat the oil in a large cast iron skillet to 350°F on a deep-frying thermometer. Fry the chicken until golden brown all over and the internal teperature reaches 165°F on a instant-read thermometer, about 4 minutes on each side.

continues

TO MAKE THE SPICED SORGHUM SYRUP

In a small saucepan, combine the bourbon, vanilla, cinnamon sticks, cloves, and orange zest over low heat. Gently simmer for 5 minutes to infuse the flavors (maintain a minimal heat to avoid any flaming of the alcohol).

Add the sorghum to the pan and gently simmer for another 10 minutes. Remove from the heat and allow the flavors to steep for 1 hour. Pass the syrup through a fine-mesh strainer and reserve. The syrup can be made up to 1 week in advance and stored in the refrigerator.

TO MAKE THE WAFFLES

Sift the cornmeal, corn flour, all-purpose flour, baking powder, baking soda, and salt together into a medium bowl.

Whisk the 3 egg yolks with the buttermilk and black pepper in a second medium bowl, then fold the egg mixture into the cornmeal mixture to create the batter. Stir the melted butter into the batter.

Whip the egg whites to stiff peaks and fold into the batter. Set aside while you start frying the chicken (see page 105).

While the chicken is frying, preheat a waffle iron. Once it is hot, spray with vegetable-oil cooking spray. Following the manufacturer's instructions, cook the waffles. They should have a crispy golden crust.

Reheat the sorghum syrup.

Serve the chicken and waffles with warm sorghum syrup and butter.

BARBECUE

Perhaps no form of American cooking is more fraught with contention than barbecue. We love to eat it, and we love to fight about it. It's found in small spots in back alleys in Chicago and on fancy menus in Memphis. It's mapped by geographers who debate the borders of South Carolina's four sauces and know where North Carolina's styles change. Wherever it is and whatever form it takes, it is one of the culinary techniques that African Americans have had a major hand in creating.

From the enslaved cooks who perfected special sauces and stayed up nights basting and turning meats they would never taste themselves to the modern-day pit masters who journey from state to state with complex rigs and secret potions to celebrate 'cue to the weekend cooks who fire up their backyard grills each summer, barbecue has long been a hallmark of American culture. African Americans have excelled at every aspect of this smoky tradition, from Maryland's bull roasts to North Carolina's pulled pork and chopped barbecue to Texas brisket, playing important roles in the creation of the myriad variations of this national culinary obsession.

Top: *Serving Barbecue at the Free Huey Rally, DeFremery Park, Oakland, California, #34, July 14, 1968*; printed 2012. Photograph by Ruth-Marion Baruch.

Bottom: Postcard of men barbecuing pork in Kentucky, early twentieth century.

HICKORY-SMOKED
BARBECUED CHICKEN

AGRICULTURAL
SOUTH

SERVES
8

ACTIVE TIME
45 MINS
🕐
TOTAL TIME
**1 DAY OR
LONGER**
REFRIGERATE
OVERNIGHT

SITTING DOWN TO FRAGRANT, juicy, hickory-smoked barbecued chicken is a southern summertime ritual.

CHEF'S NOTE

For an oven-friendly indoor version of this recipe, add 2 tablespoons smoked paprika to a cupful of the dry rub blend and follow the first two steps. The next day, roast in a preheated 275°F oven for about 1½ hours, until the chicken registers an internal temperature of 165°F on an instant-read thermometer.

2 all-natural chickens (about 3 pounds each)

1 cup Barbecue Dry Rub (see page 196)

4 cups hickory chips

4 pounds natural wood charcoal

Alabama White Barbecue Sauce (page 197), for serving

THE NIGHT BEFORE

Cut each chicken into six pieces (two legs, two thighs, and two breasts) and place them on a baking sheet.

Season the chicken pieces with the Barbecue Dry Rub, fully coating all sides. Keep the chicken on the baking sheet and place uncovered in the refrigerator overnight to marinate. Cover the hickory chips with water and leave to soak overnight.

THE NEXT DAY

Remove the chicken from the refrigerator and let it come to room temperature.

Drain the hickory chips.

To set up your smoker, first ignite the charcoal. Use an electric or chimney-style starter to avoid the unpleasant flavors associated with lighter fluid. Once the coals are fully burning and have turned white, move them to one side of the smoker. Then put the hickory chips on top of the coals to start the burning.

Set the smoker's grill rack in place and put the chicken pieces on the side that is not above the coals. Close the lid on the smoker and adjust the air supply on the bottom and the vent on the top to maintain a steady smoking temperature of 250°F. Check the cooking temperature every 30 minutes throughout the process. If the temperature drops below 250°F, you may need to add more hickory or increase the air supply. If the temperature exceeds the desired cooking temperature, reduce the air supply.

Smoke the chicken until it reaches an internal temperature of 165°F on an instant read thermometer, 3½ to 5 hours. Serve with Alabama White Barbecue Sauce.

SERVES

6 to 8

ACTIVE TIME
25 MINS
🕐
TOTAL TIME
1 DAY
PLUS
OVERNIGHT
SOAKING
OF THE
HICKORY
CHIPS

BARBECUED

BEEF BRISKET SANDWICH

IN MUCH OF THE SOUTH, barbecue is about pork. In Texas, however, beef brisket is the chosen meat on the barbecue trail. The tender, smoky beef pairs well with charred peach chutney in the Café's version of a barbecued beef brisket sandwich.

1 (5-pound) beef brisket, trimmed of excess fat (leave ¼-inch fat cap on the meat)

1 cup Barbecue Dry Rub (page 196)

1 tablespoon coarse sea salt

3 tablespoons cracked black peppercorns

10 pounds hickory wood chunks

4 pounds natural wood charcoal

6 to 8 artisanal sandwich buns, for serving

Kosher salt

Freshly ground black pepper

Charred Peach & Jalapeño Chutney (page 136), for serving

THE NIGHT BEFORE

Generously season the brisket on all sides with the Barbecue Dry Rub, sea salt, and peppercorns. Rub them thoroughly into the meat, fat, and pockets to ensure even distribution. Place the brisket on a wire rack set on top of a baking sheet. Place uncovered in the refrigerator for 12 hours to marinate.

Cover the hickory chunks with water and leave to soak overnight.

THE NEXT DAY

Remove the brisket from the refrigerator and let it to come to room temperature.

Drain the hickory chunks.

To set up your smoker, first ignite the charcoal. Use an electric or chimney-style starter to avoid the chemical flavors associated with lighter fluid. Once the coals are fully burning and have turned white, move them to one side of the smoker. Place 4 to 5 pounds (reserve the rest to replenish as needed) of the hickory chunks on top of the coals in order to start the burning.

Set the smoker's grill **rack** in place and put the brisket on it, positioning it on side that is not above the coals. The goal of setting it up like this is to create a cooking environment in which the meat is not in direct contact with the burning wood and has heat and smoke circulating around it.

Close the lid on the smoker and adjust the air supply on the bottom and vent on the top to maintain a steady smoking temperature of 230°F. Check the cooking temperature every 30 minutes throughout the process. If the temperature drops below 230°F, you may need to add more hickory or increase the air supply. If the temperature exceeds the desired cooking temperature, reduce the air supply.

After 3 hours of smoking, remove the brisket from the smoker and wrap the entire piece of meat tightly in two or three layers of aluminum foil. Then return the meat to the smoker and continue cooking. Smoke the meat until it reaches an internal temperature of 200°F on an instant-read thermometer, 5 to 6 hours longer, then allow the meat to rest for 45 minutes before slicing.

Thinly slice the brisket across the grain, generously portion the meat onto the buns, season with salt and pepper, and top with Charred Peach & Jalapeño Chutney.

SERVES
6 to **8**

ACTIVE TIME
30 MINS
⏱
TOTAL TIME
1 DAY
PLUS
OVERNIGHT
SOAKING
OF THE
HICKORY
CHIPS

HICKORY-SMOKED
PORK SHOULDER

THIS IS IT! SERVED WITH AN eastern Carolina vinegar-based sauce, this classic southern barbecued pork shoulder follows the old barbecue adage: cook it low and slow.

CHEF'S NOTE

Kettle-style smokers work well, but any smoker will do. If possible, use heritage breed pork like Berkshire or Duroc for this recipe, though good-quality supermarket pork will turn out tasty barbecue, too. Hickory chips or hardwood is a must and can be found in the grill section of most big-box stores or online.

A mop is a highly flavorful, thin basting liquid that is traditionally "mopped" on the meat periodically during the smoking process to keep the meat moist and flavorful. Here, we use a spray bottle for ease.

MOP

1 cup cider vinegar

½ cup apple juice

¼ cup vegetable oil

EASTERN NORTH CAROLINA–STYLE BARBECUE SAUCE

1½ cups cider vinegar

2 tablespoons coarsely ground black pepper

1 tablespoon red pepper flakes

1½ tablespoons sugar

1 tablespoon kosher salt

1 tablespoon Barbecue Dry Rub (page 196)

2 garlic cloves, finely chopped

MEAT

1 (5- to 6-pound) pork shoulder roast, preferably bone-in

1½ cups Barbecue Dry Rub (page 196)

10 pounds hickory wood chunks

3 pounds natural wood charcoal

TO MAKE THE MOP

Mix together all the ingredients, and reserve at room temperature for the smoking process.

TO MAKE THE BARBECUE SAUCE

Combine the vinegar, black pepper, red pepper flakes, sugar, salt, and Barbecue Dry Rub in a medium bowl and mix well. Stir in the garlic. Cover and refrigerate.

Allow the sauce to develop for at least 12 hours before serving to ensure maximum flavor. It will keep refrigerated for up to 2 weeks.

THE DAY BEFORE

Using plenty of paper towels, throughly dry the entire surface of the pork shoulder. This will ensure better seasoning of the meat.

Place the shoulder on a baking sheet and generously season on all sides with the Barbecue Dry Rub. Be sure to rub it into the meat, fat, and pockets to ensure even distribution. Place the meat on a wire rack set on a baking sheet. Place uncovered in the refrigerator 12 hours to marinate.

Cover hickory chunks with water and leave to soak overnight.

Remove the pork shoulder from the refrigerator and let it come to room temperature.

Drain the hickory chunks.

To set up your smoker, first ignite the charcoal. Use an electric or chimney-style starter to avoid the chemical flavors associated with lighter fluid.

Once the coals are fully burning and have turned white, move them to one side of the smoker. Place 4 to 5 pounds (reserve the rest to replenish as needed) of the hickory chunks on top of the coals in order to start the burning.

Set the smoker's grill rack in place and put the pork shoulder on it, positioning it to the side that is not above the coals. The goal of setting it up like this is to create a cooking environment in which the meat is not in direct contact with the burning wood and has heat and smoke circulating around it.

Close the lid on the smoker and adjust the air supply on the bottom and vent on the top to maintain a smoking temperature of 220°F. Check the cooking temperature every 30 minutes throughout the process. If the temperature drops below 220°F, you may need to add more hickory or increase the air supply. If the temperature exceeds the desired cooking temperature, reduce the air supply.

Every 45 to 60 minutes give the meat a quick spray with the mop sauce to help keep it moist and flavorful.

Smoke the meat for up to 6 to 8 hours, until it reaches an internal temperature of 190°F on an instant-read thermometer. Let the meat rest for 45 minutes before beginning to pull it. Pulling can be done either by shredding the meat using one fork in each hand or by simply pulling it apart with your fingers.

Once the meat has been pulled, season it with the barbecue sauce and with salt and pepper to taste if needed.

SERVES

4

ACTIVE TIME
25 MINS

🕐

TOTAL TIME
45 MINS

PAN-ROASTED PORK CHOPS

THIS DISH OF BACON-WRAPPED pork chops is a testament to the belief that if one type of pork is tasty in a dish, two types are surely better. Here, in addition to the smoky bacon, the chops draw flavor from the addition of thyme sprigs as they cook and from the molasses gravy that finishes the dish.

4 (2-inch-thick) bone-in pork chops, preferably heritage-breed pork such as Berkshire

4 bacon slices, preferably hardwood-smoked

1½ teaspoons kosher salt

Freshly ground black pepper

8 fresh thyme sprigs

1 tablespoon olive oil

2 garlic cloves, lightly crushed

2 teaspoons shallot, finely diced

2 teaspoons sherry vinegar

2 tablespoons unsulfured molasses

1 tablespoon cracked black peppercorns

1 cup Brown Sauce (page 100)

2 teaspoons unsalted butter

Coarse sea salt

Remove the pork chops and bacon from the refrigerator and let come to room temperature.

Season the chops on both sides with the salt and a quick grind or two of black pepper. Place 2 thyme sprigs on each chop. Stretch a bacon slice over the thyme and around each chop. As the chop cooks, the bacon will help baste the pork while the thyme perfumes the meat.

Heat the olive oil in a large skillet over medium heat. When the oil begins to shimmer, increase the heat to high and place each chop, with the overlapping bacon edges facing down, in the pan. Add the garlic to the pan and allow to remain throughout the cooking process.

Brown the chops on the first side for 3 to 4 minutes, until a golden brown crust has formed. Turn the chops over and brown the second side for 3 to 4 minutes. Remove the chops and set aside to rest while the sauce is being finished.

Add the shallot to the skillet and sauté lightly over medium heat. Add the sherry vinegar and loosen any bits from the bottom of the pan with a wooden spoon. Add the molasses and cracked peppercorns, followed by the Brown Sauce. Cook over high heat until the liquid has reduced by half, about 2 minutes. To finish, remove the garlic cloves and discard, then whisk the butter into the sauce.

Serve the chops with a generous amount of the molasses gravy and a sprinkling of sea salt.

PORK RIBS

✖

THIS RECIPE WAS DEVELOPED to celebrate the Café's first participation in the Washington, DC, National Cherry Blossom Festival. The festival celebrates the blooming of the more than three thousand cherry trees that originated as a gift from the mayor of Tokyo, Japan, to the United States in 1912. The use of such ingredients as *shichimi togarashi*, a Japanese spice mixture, and Asian pears gives these succulent, tender ribs a delicious Asian flavor.

2 Asian pears, peeled, cored, and pureed

2 tablespoons packed light brown sugar

¼ cup soy sauce

¼ cup oyster sauce

1 tablespoon rice wine

¼ teaspoon kosher salt

1½ teaspoons shichimi togarashi (Japanese chili pepper spice blend, available in most Asian markets)

4 garlic cloves, finely chopped

½ cup sweet chile sauce

1½ teaspoons grated and peeled fresh ginger

½ tablespoon five-spice powder

5 pounds St. Louis–style pork ribs

3 to 4 pounds cherry wood chunks, for smoking the ribs

1 scallion, white and light green parts, thinly sliced, for garnish

THE NIGHT BEFORE

Combine the pear puree, sugar, soy sauce, oyster sauce, rice wine, salt, shichimi togarashi, garlic, chile sauce, ginger, and five-spice powder in a 2-quart saucepan.

Place over medium heat, stirring until it comes to a boil. Reduce the heat to a low simmer and cook until slightly thickened, about 15 minutes.

Remove from the heat and allow to cool to room temperature, about 30 minutes.

Once the sauce has cooled, pour it over the ribs, coating them completely. Cover the ribs and place in the refrigerator to marinate for 12 to 24 hours.

THE NEXT DAY

Drain the ribs, reserving the marinade. Pass the marinade through a fine-mesh strainer and reserve.

To set up your smoker, first ignite the charcoal. Use an electric or chimney-style starter to avoid the unpleasant flavors associated with lighter fluid. Once the coals are fully burning and have turned white, move them to one side of the smoker. Put 3 pounds of the cherry wood chips on top of the coals to start the burning.

Set the smoker's grill rack in place and put the ribs on the side that is not above the coals. Close the lid on the smoker and adjust the air supply on the bottom and the vent on the top to maintain a steady smoking temperature of 275°F.

Check the cooking temperature
every 30 minutes throughout the
process. Smoke the ribs until they
reach an internal temperature of
200°F oon an instant-read thermometer, about 2½ hours.

Brush the ribs with the reserved
marinade and cook for another
10 minutes until well glazed and
sticky. Garnish with the scallion
before serving.

CURRIED GOAT

CULINARY
COUSINS

SERVES
4 to **6**

ACTIVE TIME
40 MINS
○
TOTAL TIME
1 DAY
PLUS
REFRIGERATE
MARINATED
GOAT
OVERNIGHT

IN JAMAICA, CURRIED GOAT is a traditional favorite. The dish originated with the island's East Indian community, today the country's third largest racial group. Their ancestors arrived as indentured workers in the post-emancipation period, mainly to work on sugarcane plantations. This curry is also a tasty way to deal with the numerous goats that roam the island's countryside.

CHEF'S NOTE
Rich with Madras-style curry powder, which flavors much of the island's Indian cooking, this dish also includes traditional Caribbean herbs and spices, such as Scotch bonnet peppers, and can be made with mutton or lamb if goat is unavailable.

1 large white onion, chopped

2 scallions, white and light green parts, chopped

4 garlic cloves, finely chopped

1 tablespoon fresh ginger, peeled and chopped

4 whole allspice berries

4 tablespoons peanut oil, divided

3 pounds boneless goat stew meat, cut into 2-inch cubes

1 tablespoon plus 2 teaspoons curry powder

1 tablespoon kosher salt

1 teaspoon freshly ground black pepper

1½ teapoons ground cumin

1½ teaspoon ground coriander

¼ teaspoon ground ginger

4 quarts Chicken Stock (page 200)

1 bay leaf

3 fresh thyme sprigs

1 cinnamon stick

1½ cups potato, peeled and diced

1 cup carrot, peeled and diced

1 Scotch bonnet, habanero, or jalapeño pepper, halved and seeded

THE NIGHT BEFORE
In a blender, puree the onion, scallions, garlic, fresh ginger, allspice, and 2 tablespoons of the oil until a smooth mixture is formed. Put the goat meat in a large bowl and mix with the puree until the meat is well coated. Place in an airtight container and refrigerate overnight.

THE NEXT DAY
To make the spice blend, combine the curry powder, salt, pepper, cumin, coriander, and ground ginger in a small bowl. Mix until well blended.

Heat the remaining 2 tablespoons oil in a large stockpot over medium heat. Add the goat meat and its marinade and brown well on all sides. Then add the curry spice blend and cook for another 3 minutes, stirring regularly.

Next add the Chicken Stock and bring to a boil. Reduce the temperature to maintain a simmer, add the bay leaf, thyme, and cinnamon, cover, and cook gently for 45 to 60 minutes, until meat is fork tender. Skim off excess fat from the surface.

Now add the potatoes, carrots, and Scotch bonnet pepper, and simmer for another 25 to 30 minutes, until the goat and vegetables are tender.

With a slotted spoon, remove the meat and vegetables and reserve. Continue cooking the braising liquid for another 15 minutes to reduce. Skim off any additional fat. Adjust the seasoning with salt and pepper.

Remove the bay leaf, return the meat and vegetables to the sauce, and reheat. Serve over rice.

SERVES

6

ACTIVE TIME
20 MINS

TOTAL TIME
40 MINS

LIMPIN' SUSAN

❀

IN GULLAH FOLKLORE, LIMPIN' Susan is often referred to as Hoppin' John's wife. This okra and rice purloo (pilaf) is also found in Guadeloupe, where it is called *riz aux gombos*. In the Low Country, it is often paired with sautéed shrimp.

4 thick bacon slices, diced

¼ cup yellow onion, minced

1 garlic clove, finely chopped

2½ cups okra, cut into
¼-inch-thick rounds

1 teaspoon kosher salt

½ teaspoon freshly ground
black pepper

1 pinch cayenne pepper

2 bay leaves

1 cup Carolina Gold rice or
other long-grain white rice

2½ cups Chicken Stock
(page 200)

3 scallions, white and light
green parts, thinly sliced

Preheat a soup pot over medium-low heat. Cook the bacon in the pot until it renders its fat and is crisp. Using a slotted spoon transfer the bacon to a plate.

Add the onion and garlic to the pot and cook over medium heat until translucent, about 5 minutes. Then add the okra, salt, black pepper, cayenne, and bay leaves and cook for another 5 minutes, stirring continually.

Now add the rice to the pot and stir until all the grains are well coated with the vegetables. Pour in the Chicken Stock and bring to a simmer. Cover, reduce the heat to low, and cook until the rice is tender and the liquid is absorbed, 18 to 20 minutes.

Garnish with the scallions and bacon before serving.

TRINI DOUBLES

CULINARY COUSINS

SERVES
4 to **6**

ACTIVE TIME
25 MINS
🕐
TOTAL TIME
1 DAY
PLUS OVERNIGHT SOAKING OF THE CHICKPEAS

VEGETARIAN

TRINIDADIAN STREET FOOD IS some of the best in the Caribbean and shows off that nation's African, Asian, European, and Native American roots. The East Indian influence is evidenced in doubles, which are two pieces of fried dough, known as *bara* (similar to roti), filled with curry *channa* (curried chickpeas) and topped with a variety of condiments, including the fiery local hot sauce.

CHEF'S NOTE

West Indian hot pepper sauce has a different flavor profile from most hot sauces in the United States. Look for it online.

8 ounces dried chickpeas (rounded 1 cup)

¼ cup vegetable oil

1 cup yellow onion, minced

3 garlic cloves, smashed

1½ teaspoons ground turmeric

2½ tablespoons curry powder

1 tablespoon garam masala

1 bay leaf

1 habanero pepper, halved lengthwise

2 cups yellow potatoes, peeled and finely diced

¼ cup fresh cilantro, chopped, plus sprigs for serving

Salt

Freshly ground black pepper

Roti (page 156), for serving

1 cucumber, thinly shaved, for serving

West Indian hot pepper sauce, for serving

THE NIGHT BEFORE

Sort through the chickpeas to remove any debris and stones. Place the chickpeas in a colander and rinse under cold water. Transfer to a large soup pot and cover with cold water. The water level should reach at least 2 inches above the chickpeas. Leave to soak overnight.

THE NEXT DAY

Drain and rinse the chickpeas, then place them in a medium soup pot and fully cover with water. Bring to a full boil, then reduce to a steady simmer and cook for about 45 minutes, until tender. Drain the chickpeas and reserve the chickpeas and cooking liquid separately.

In the soup pot, heat the vegetable oil over medium heat. Add the onion and garlic and cook until translucent, about 5 minutes. Add the turmeric, curry powder, and garam masala and cook until the mixture becomes aromatic and begins to darken slightly, 2 to 3 minutes.

Add the chickpeas, bay leaf, habanero, potatoes, and about 1½ cups of the chickpea cooking liquid and bring to a boil. Lower the heat and simmer until the potatoes are soft, about 20 minutes.

Once the mixture is cooked, remove the habanero pepper and bay leaf, and add the chopped cilantro. Season to taste with salt and pepper.

Serve the chickpeas over freshly cooked Roti and top with the cucumber, cilantro sprigs, and hot pepper sauce.

MAKES

12

EMPANADAS

ACTIVE TIME

1 HR

🕐

TOTAL TIME

2 HRS

VEGETARIAN

BLACK-EYED PEA, GOLDEN CORN, & CHANTERELLE
EMPANADAS

✠

IN THE LATIN AMERICAN world, an empanada is a turnover filled with various ingredients. Here, the savory pastry conceals a mixture of black-eyed peas, grilled corn, and chanterelle mushrooms that speaks of the African American and Native American cultures of the Western Range.

CHEF'S NOTE
Empanada wrappers can be found in Hispanic markets or online.

FRESH TOMATO SALSA
¾ cup vine-ripened tomatoes, diced

½ cup extra-virgin olive oil

¼ cup fresh cilantro leaves, coarsely chopped

¼ cup red onion, minced

2 tablespoons freshly squeezed lime juice

½ teaspoon kosher salt

Freshly ground black pepper

EMPANADAS
1 ear corn

1 tablespoon olive oil, divided

2 shallots, finely diced

1 garlic clove, chopped into a paste

½ teaspoon ground cumin

12 ounces fresh chanterelles or other wild mushrooms, sliced

¾ teaspoon kosher salt

Freshly ground black pepper

1 cup cooked black-eyed peas

1 tablespoon fresh flat-leaf parsley, chopped

¼ teaspoon fresh thyme leaves

12 (6-inch) empanada wrappers

3 cups vegetable oil, for frying

TO MAKE THE TOMATO SALSA
Mix all the ingredients together in a small bowl and marinate for at least 2 hours.

TO MAKE FOR THE EMPANADAS
While the Fresh Tomato Salsa is marinating, make the empanadas. Shuck the corn. Use a serrated knife to cut the kernels from the cob. You should have about 1 cup kernels. Heat a 10-inch cast iron skillet over high heat. Add a few drops of the olive oil and the corn. Cook, stirring, until the kernels are fragrant and begin to char, about 2 to 3 minutes. Transfer the kernels to a small bowl.

Return the skillet to the stovetop, add the remaining oil, and heat over medium heat. Add the shallots and garlic and cook until translucent, about 5 minutes. About halfway through the cooking, stir in the cumin. Add the chanterelles and cook for 3 more minutes. Season with the salt and pepper to taste.

While the chanterelles are cooking, roughly chop ¼ cup of the black-eyed peas to a mash consistency. Add the corn kernels and chopped black-eyed peas to the chanterelles and cook for 2 more minutes. Transfer to a medium bowl and set aside to cool.

Once the mixture has cooled, fold in the remaining black-eyed peas and the parsley and thyme. Taste and adjust the seasoning with salt and pepper if necessary.

Place an empanada wrapper on a work surface and spoon 3 generous tablespoons of the mixture onto one side of the wrapper. Wet a pastry brush with water and moisten the outside edge of the wrapper. Fold the blank side over the filling, pressing the edges to seal the empanada. With floured fork tines, lightly press around the edge of the empanada to seal it securely. Repeat this process until all the filling and empanada wrappers have been used. Refrigerate for 30 minutes prior to cooking.

In a deep cast iron skillet, heat the vegetable oil to 350°F on a deep-frying thermometer. Working in batches to avoid crowding, add the empanadas to the hot oil and fry, turning once, until crisp and a rich golden brown color, about 3 to 4 minutes total. Using tongs or a slotted spoon, transfer to a platter lined with paper towels to drain any excess oil.

Serve hot with Fresh Tomato Salsa.

PICKLES,
SNACKS,
AND
BREADS

Top left: A picnic, mid-twentieth century.

Top middle: Fork and knife from the home of Harriet Tubman, ca. 1870s.

Bottom middle: Students working in a kitchen at the Bordentown School in Bordentown, New Jersey, ca. 1935. Photograph by Lewis Wickes Hine.

Opposite right: Teapot made by Peter Bentzon, ca. 1817–29.

PIMENTO CHEESE

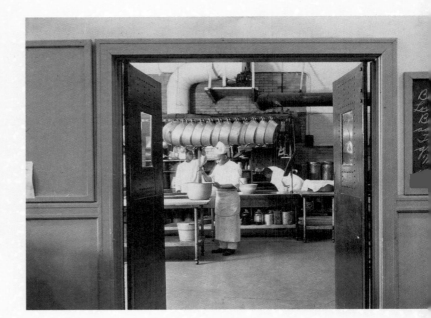

**PICKLES, CHUTNEY,
AND CHOW-CHOW**

PICKLES, SNACKS, AND BREADS

Feature: Culinary Cousins / 128

Pickled Watermelon Rind / 131

Feature: Watermelon / 132

Dilly Green Beans / 133

Spicy Pickled Okra / 134

Chow-Chow / 135

Charred Peach & Jalapeño Chutney / 136

Deviled Eggs / 137

Pimento Cheese / 139

Sea Salt–Spiced Cocktail Nuts / 140

Creole Spiced Boiled Peanuts / 141

Black-Eyed Pea Hummus / 142

Feature: Peas / 143

Texas Caviar / 144

Sweet Onion & Corn Hush Puppies
with Red Pepper Remoulade / 146

"Cracklin'" Corn Bread / 147

Johnnycakes / 149

Hot Water Corn Bread / 150

Yellow Corn Bread / 151

Buttermilk Biscuits / 152

Drop Biscuits / 153

Sweet Potato Biscuits / 155

Roti / 156

Benne Seed Flatbread Crisps / 157

CULINARY COUSINS

Anyone who has family knows that cousins are complicated. Some cousins are as close as brothers or sisters; others are distant but display startling family resemblances; and still others know their relationships but have few connections. With matters culinary, cousins are the same: some are immediately identifiable as sharing a close relationship, such as West Africa's Joloff rice and the red rice of the South Carolina Low Country. Their kinship with jambalaya from New Orleans may be a little more distant, but it is certainly evident on the plate and the palate. And all three are related to *thiebou dienn*, the Senegalese national dish of red rice and fish that inspired the original Joloff rice.

Just as red rice and jambalaya are closely related to their African cousins, so too is Hoppin' John. South Carolina's black-eyed pea and rice pilaf is much like Senegal's *thiebou niébé*, which boasts the same combination of black-eyed peas and rice but is seasoned with beef or smoked mollusks instead of the South's traditional smoked pork.

Fritters are everywhere, from those fashioned from leftover vegetables in the Agricultural South to the bean fritters of Brazil and the salt cod fritters of the Caribbean. Finally, there are the gumbos: rich soups filled with the bounty of coastal regions that may be thickened with okra or filé. These soupy stews share connections with the *sauce feuilles* of Benin and the *soupikandia* of the Diola of Senegal and are cousins to the *callaloos* of the Caribbean and even the pepper pot of Philadelphia. All are testimonials to the myriad ways in which the culinary cultures of the African Atlantic world have mixed and mingled on the plate.

These culinary relations look backward to where African Americans have been and forward to the interrelated culinary worlds of the African diaspora. They include foods from Senegal, Ghana, Guyana, Salvador da Bahia, Brazil, and the American places where Africans and the continent's descendants, old and new, have landed and transformed their food into American classics.

Opposite top: Postcard of women carrying produce in Jamaica, late nineteenth to early twentieth century.

"Greetings from Jamaica"
Going to Market with Yams
and Canes, Constant Spring Road

STICKY PORK RIBS

PICKLED
WATERMELON RIND

MAKES

1 qt.

ACTIVE TIME
20 MINS

🕐

TOTAL TIME
30 MINS
PLUS
1-DAY
PICKLING
TIME

THESE ICONIC PICKLES ARE prepared from the peeled white rind of the fruit that is usually discarded. In Harlem, during the Great Depression, an African American woman named Patsy Randolph would go from shop to shop collecting watermelon rinds that she would then transform into pickles. She sold her home-made pickles with great success, in yet another demonstration of the marriage of African American culinary abilities and entrepreneurial skills to create capital.

CHEF'S NOTE

At the Café, star anise is used in the pickling mix, which gives the pickles a slightly Asian flavor. The pickles can be made up to a week in advance and stored in the refrigerator until ready to use.

1 (4- to 5-pound) watermelon

2 ounces fresh ginger, peeled and sliced

2 cinnamon sticks

4 whole allspice berries

4 whole cloves

1 teaspoon black peppercorns

3 whole star anise

1½ tablespoons kosher salt

1 jalapeño pepper, thinly sliced

1 cup sugar

1 cup distilled white vinegar

¾ cup cold water

Prepare a 1-quart Mason jar, lid, and screwband by throughly washing and drying them.

With a sharp vegetable peeler, remove the thick green rind from the watermelon.

Cut the watermelon into 1½-inch-thick slices and then trim the flesh, leaving about ¼ inch of red flesh attached to the rind. Cut the rind into 1½-inch pieces. You should end up with about 4½ cups rind. Reserve the rest of the watermelon for another use, such as heirloom Tomato-Watermelon Salad (page 20).

In a medium saucepan, combine the ginger, cinnamon, allspice, cloves, peppercorns, star anise, salt, jalapeño, sugar, vinegar, and water. Bring to a boil over high heat. Reduce the heat to a simmer, add the watermelon rind, and cook for 5 minutes.

Remove from the heat and allow to cool to room temperature. Make sure the watermelon rind is completely covered by the brine. A small salad plate can be placed on top of the rind to keep it submerged.

Once fully cooled, transfer the rind to the prepared jar and pour in enough brine to cover it completely. Close the jar with the lid and screwband. Refrigerate for 24 hours prior to serving. Consume within 7 days for optimum freshness and flavor.

Clockwise from top left: Chow-Chow, Charred Peach & Jalapeño Chutney, Dilly Green Beans, Spicy Pickled Okra, and Pickled Watermelon Rind

WATERMELON

"Watermelon, sweet to the rind / If you don't believe me, then pull down your blind! / Watermelon! Watermelon!" This street vendor's cry, recorded in the mid-twentieth century, is testimonial to the enduring popularity of the bright red fruit that is summer's favorite treat, complete with juice dripping down chins and seed-spitting contests.

The watermelon originated on the African continent, and Egyptians began cultivating it early, as evidenced by images of the fruit and its seeds on the walls of tombs dating back at least four thousand years, including the famed resting place of King Tutankhamun. The fruit was introduced to Spain by the Moors, and Spaniards and enslaved Africans carried it to the New World, where it was recorded growing in Florida in the sixteenth century and in Massachusetts in the early seventeenth century.

Watermelon was especially prized in areas where the water supply was of uncertain purity or nonexistent, as the plant is 92 percent liquid and can quench thirst. This certainly meant survival for enslaved folk working in the hot sun. However, the often lifesaving love of watermelon has been a double-edged sword for African Americans. Some of the most virulently negative images of the late nineteenth and early twentieth centuries involve racist stereotyping of African American love of the fruit.

Most of that has now passed, and each summer brings out a host of self-proclaimed watermelon specialists, who thump, prod, and poke to select the sweetest, juiciest watermelons to take to countless occasions for the delectation of all.

Above: *Untitled*, ca. 1940. A man sells watermelon from the back of a truck in Harlem, New York. From the series *Most Crowded Block in the World*. Photograph by Aaron Siskind.

DILLY
GREEN BEANS

MAKES
2 pts.

ACTIVE TIME
20 MINS
🕐
TOTAL TIME
25 MINS
PLUS
2-DAYS
PICKLING
TIME

HERE IS AN INVENTIVE—and delicious—way to prepare a bumper crop of summer green beans. They can be eaten as a snack, added to salads, or used as a garnish in dishes or drinks.

1 pound green beans

½ bunch fresh dill with stems

6 garlic cloves, thinly sliced

2 cups distilled white vinegar

2 tablespoons kosher salt

2 tablespoons sugar

1 tablespoon black peppercorns

1 tablespoon yellow mustard seeds

1 teaspoon coriander seeds

2 small dried hot red peppers

Prepare two (1-pint) Mason jars, lids, and screwband by throughly washing and drying them.

Wash and trim the green beans so they will fit in the jars. Pack the beans, standing up, dill, and garlic into the prepared jars.

Combine the vinegar, salt, sugar, peppercorns, mustard seeds, coriander seeds, and peppers in a saucepan and bring to a boil. Pour the hot brine and spices into the jars with the beans.

Cover the jars with lids and screwbands. Let cool to room temperature, then refrigerate. The beans need 2 to 3 days to develop their best flavor. They will keep in the refrigerator for up to 3 weeks.

SERVES
6 to 8

ACTIVE TIME
30 MINS
○
TOTAL TIME
35 MINS
PLUS
2-DAYS
PICKLING
TIME

SPICY
PICKLED OKRA

OKRA PLANTS ARE BEAUTIFUL growing in a garden and look much like their botanical relative, the hibiscus. They are at their peak in the South in the late summer and early fall, when an abundance of green pods appears. That's also a good time to prepare a batch or two of these hot and spicy okra pickles.

CHEF'S NOTE

For the best results when pickling, use only kosher salt or pickling salt.

2 pounds okra

6 garlic cloves

10 red Thai peppers

½ cup pearl onions, peeled

2 cups distilled white vinegar

1 cup water

2 tablespoons kosher or pickling salt

1 tablespoon sugar

1 teaspoon ground turmeric

1 tablespoon yellow mustard seeds

1 tablespoon coriander seeds

1 teaspoon celery seeds

Prepare a 1-quart Mason jar, lid, and screwband by throughly washing and drying them (or use two or three 1-pint jars).

Leave the okra pods intact. Peel the garlic cloves, cut them in half lengthwise, and remove any green sprouts. Set aside. Split the peppers in half lengthwise. Set aside separately.

Fill the jar with the okra, placing the first layer stem-side down and the next layer stem-side up. (This will maximize the number of okra pods that will fit in the jar.) Between each layer of okra, add the garlic, Thai peppers, and pearl onions. Fill the jar just past its shoulders, or about 2 inches from the lip.

In a small stainless steel pot, combine the vinegar, water, salt, sugar, turmeric, and mustard, coriander, and celery seeds. Bring to a boil, reduce to a simmer, and cook for 3 minutes.

While the brine is still hot, pour it into the jars, fully covering the okra and filling to within ¼ inch of the lip. Insert a thin knife into the jar and gently stir two or three times to ensure that no air bubbles remain. Close the jar with the lid and screwband. Let cool to room temperature, then refrigerate. Pickled okra needs 2 to 3 days to develop flavor and can be held in the refrigerator for up to 3 weeks.

CHOW-CHOW

AGRICULTURAL SOUTH

MAKES

2 qts.

ACTIVE TIME
35 MINS

TOTAL TIME
1 DAY
PLUS REFRIGERATE OVERNIGHT

IN HER 1881 BOOK *WHAT MRS. Fisher Knows about Old Southern Cooking*, Abby Fisher, a former slave who became a pickle and preserve maker in San Francisco (see page 56), included two recipes for chow-chow. One is traditional and calls for cabbage, and the other is called Creole chow-chow and uses green tomatoes.

CHEF'S NOTE

The Café's chow-chow uses both cabbage and green tomato to create a condiment that can be a side dish at a picnic or barbecue or a topping for a burger or sandwich.

2 cups Videlia or other sweet onion, finely diced

1 cup green bell pepper, finely diced

1 cup red bell pepper, finely diced

1 jalapeño pepper, seeded and finely chopped

½ head green cabbage, ribs removed and finely diced

4 cups cored green tomatoes, finely diced

⅓ cup kosher salt

1½ cups sugar

1 tablespoon ground turmeric

2 tablespoons yellow mustard seeds

1 tablespoon black mustard seeds

1 teaspoon celery seeds

3 whole cloves

¼ teaspoon red pepper flakes

4 cups distilled white vinegar

THE NIGHT BEFORE

Put the onion, green and red bell peppers, jalapeño, cabbage, and tomatoes in a large stainless steel bowl. Add the salt and mix until the salt is well distributed throughout the vegetables. Cover and refrigerate overnight.

THE NEXT DAY

Prepare two (1-quart) Mason jars, lids, and screwbands by throughly washing and drying them.

Transfer the marinated vegetables to a colander and allow the excess water to drain.

Combine the sugar, turmeric, yellow and black mustard seeds, celery seeds, cloves, red pepper flakes, and vinegar in a medium stockpot and bring to a boil over high heat. Reduce the heat and simmer for 5 minutes. Add the drained vegetables to the brine and cook for another 5 minutes.

Pour the vegetables and brine into the prepared Mason jars, making sure the vegetables are fully covered with the brine. Close the jars with the lids and screwbands. Let cool to room temperature, then refrigerate. Allow the flavors to mature for 2 to 3 days prior to serving. The pickle will keep in the refrigerator for up to 2 weeks.

CHARRED PEACH
AND JALAPEÑO CHUTNEY

WHEN MANY PEOPLE THINK of peaches, they typically think of Georgia, but the West has its peaches, too, including areas of Colorado where they have been growing the fruit since the nineteenth century. This flavorful chutney combines the juicy sweetness of the fruit with the heat of jalapeño peppers.

6 ripe peaches

1 tablespoon vegetable oil

¼ cup Vidalia or sweet onion, diced

1 jalapeño pepper, seeded and minced

2 tablespoons fresh ginger, peeled and grated

½ cup honey, preferably Western wildflower

2 tablespoons packed light brown sugar

2 tablespoons sherry vinegar

2 tablespoons fresh cilantro leaves, chopped

1 pinch kosher salt

Freshly ground black pepper

Fill a medium stockpot with water and bring to a boil. Prepare a large bowl of ice water. With a paring knife, cut a quarter-sized X, in the bottom of each peach. Place the peaches in the boiling water for 30 seconds, then, using a slotted spoon, transfer them to the bowl of ice water.

Let cool, then gently remove the skin, cut the peaches in half, and remove the pits.

Prepare a hot fire in a charcoal or gas grill or preheat a cast iron skillet over high heat. Once it has become extremely hot, add the peaches, cut-side down, and allow them to char for about 1½ minutes. Once the peaches have developed a rich charred color, remove them and set aside.

In a large sauté pan, heat the vegetable oil over medium heat, Add the onion and cook until translucent, about 5 minutes. While the onion is cooking, cut the peaches into 2-inch chunks, preserving the charred bits.

When the onion is ready, add the jalapeño and ginger and cook for 1 minute longer. Add the honey and brown sugar, increase the heat to high, and bring quickly to a boil. Stir in the vinegar, reduce the heat to medium, and simmer for 1 minute. Add the peaches and cook for about 5 minutes.

Remove from the heat, transfer the peaches and syrup to a bowl, and let cool to room temperature. Once cool, add the cilantro. Season with the salt and pepper.

Store the chutney in an airtight container in the refrigerator for up to 5 days.

DEVILED EGGS

AGRICULTURAL
SOUTH

MAKES

2 doz.

EGGS

ACTIVE TIME
30 MINS

🕐

TOTAL TIME
45 MINS

WRAPPED IN WAXED PAPER, deviled eggs journeyed north and west with African Americans leaving the South during the Great Migration. Today, as in the past, they are slipped into fancy deviled-egg plates and set on formal tables and turn up at picnics almost as frequently as ants.

CHEF'S NOTE

The Café adds pimento cheese to the yolk mixture and garnishes the finished eggs with snipped chives and bacon.

12 large eggs

1 teaspoon kosher salt, plus more for seasoning

2 teaspoons Dijon mustard

1 tablespoon mayonnaise, preferably Duke's

2 dashes Tabasco sauce

¾ cup Pimento Cheese (page 139)

2 tablespoons snipped fresh chives

5 hardwood-smoked bacon slices, fried crisp

Place the eggs in a saucepan with the 1 teaspoon salt. Add cold water to cover by 1 inch. Bring to a full simmer uncovered. Remove the pan from the heat, cover, and let stand for 15 minutes. Meanwhile, prepare a large bowl of ice water.

Using a slotted spoon, transfer the hard-boiled **eggs** to the ice water and leave to cool for 10 minutes.

Peel the eggs and slice in half lengthwise, removing the yolks to a medium bowl. Set the whites, hollow-side up, on a serving plate.

With the back of a fork, mash the cooked yolks into a paste, gradually adding the mustard, mayonnaise, Tabasco sauce, and Pimento Cheese. Stir until well blended.

Place the yolk filling in a pastry bag fitted with a large star tip. Pipe the mixture into the egg whites. Garnish each deviled egg with the chives and a small piece of crisp bacon.

PIMENTO CHEESE

AGRICULTURAL
SOUTH

MAKES

4 cups

ACTIVE TIME
20 MINS

TOTAL TIME
20 MINS

AN ICONIC SOUTHERN SNACK food, pimento cheese turns up everywhere from fancy buffets to informal gatherings. Although the traditional version uses sharp Cheddar, cooks are experimenting with different cheeses and coming up with their own spins on this southern favorite.

CHEF'S NOTE
For best results, use a mayonnaise with no added sugar.

1 pound cream cheese, at room temperature

¾ cup mayonnaise, preferably Duke's

¾ cup pimentos, preferably freshly roasted and peeled, or jarred Spanish piquillo peppers, cut into tiny dice

1 teaspoon hot sauce

½ teaspoon sugar

¼ teaspoon smoked paprika (*piminton*)

1 pinch cayenne pepper

¾ teaspoon kosher salt

¼ teaspoon freshly ground white pepper

1¼ pounds aged sharp Vermont Cheddar cheese, coarsely grated

In a medium bowl, stir the softened cream cheese with a stiff whisk until smooth. Add the mayonnaise and continue mixing until both ingredients are fully blended into a uniform consistency.

Add the pimentos, hot sauce, sugar, paprika, cayenne, salt, and pepper and mix to blend well.

Gently fold in the Cheddar and mix to distribute the cheese evenly. Avoid overmixing; the cheese should remain in coarse pieces.

Transfer to a container with a lid. Store in the refrigerator for up to 3 days.

MAKES

4 cups

ACTIVE TIME
15 MINS

TOTAL TIME
1 HR

SEA SALT–SPICED
COCKTAIL NUTS

THESE MAY BE CALLED cocktail nuts, but this sweet and spicy mixture tastes just as good when eaten as a between-meal or late-night snack. One of the featured nuts, pecans, is a species of hickory nut native to the southern United States. Pronunciations of this popular nut vary; some people pronounce it "pehcan" and others say "pee-can." Whatever you call them, they're delicious, especially in this mix.

CHEF'S NOTE

Benne is another word for sesame seeds.

½ cup granulated sugar	1 cup jumbo cashews
¼ cup packed light brown sugar	1 cup whole blanched almonds
1 tablespoon sea salt	1 cup jumbo pecan halves
1 tablespoon smoked paprika	½ cup whole blanched hazelnuts
2 teaspoons ground cinnamon	½ cup walnut halves
2 teaspoons cayenne pepper	¼ cup benne (sesame) seeds
1 large egg white	1 tablespoon unsulfured molasses

Preheat the oven to 300°F.

Line a rimmed baking sheet with a nonstick silicone mat or parchment paper coated with vegetable-oil cooking spray.

In a small bowl, stir together both sugars, salt, paprika, cinnamon, and cayenne. In a large bowl, whisk the egg white until light and frothy. Fold in the cashews, almonds, pecans, hazelnuts, walnuts, benne seeds, sugar-spice blend, and molasses. Toss well until the nuts are fully coated.

Spread the nuts in a single layer on the prepared baking sheet. Bake the nuts, stirring occasionally to ensure they are toasting evenly, until they are a rich golden, about 45 minutes.

Allow the nuts to cool on the baking sheet, then store in an airtight container at room temperature for up to 3 days.

CREOLE SPICED
BOILED PEANUTS

SERVES
8 to **10**

ACTIVE TIME
30 MINS

⊙

TOTAL TIME
**8 HRS
30 MINS**

BOILED PEANUTS ARE AN autumn treat in the South, with their slippery texture making them something like the local version of edamame. They are especially prized in Charleston, South Carolina, where they were sold by one of the city's last street hawkers, the late Anthony Wright, known as Tony the Peanut Man, who died in 2016. His rhyming cry was a throwback to an earlier generation of African American street vendors.

CHEF'S NOTE

It is best to cook these peanuts outdoors, as the cooking process generates a lot of heat. A common turkey fryer kit over a propane burner offers the perfect setup.

5 pounds fresh green peanuts in the shell

½ cup Creole Spice Blend (page 196)

¼ cup kosher salt

¼ cup hot sauce

3 tablespoons turbinado sugar

12 quarts cold water

Sort through the peanuts to remove any stems and debris. Wash them twice in cold water.

Transfer the cleaned peanuts to a large stockpot. Add the Creole Spice Blend, salt, hot sauce, and sugar. Cover with the water, bring to a boil, and boil for about 8 hours. During the cooking process replenish the water as needed to keep the original level.

The peanuts are done when they float to the top and are soft and tender to the bite. Scoop them out of the brine and enjoy while hot. You can cook the peanuts a day or two in advance, but they must be immediately cooled and stored in their brine in the refrigerator.

SERVES

4 to 6

ACTIVE TIME
10 MINS

TOTAL TIME
45 MINS
PLUS
OVERNIGHT
SOAKING
OF THE
BLACK-EYED
PEAS

VEGETARIAN

BLACK-EYED PEA
HUMMUS

HUMMUS, THE TRADITIONAL Middle Eastern spread of ground chickpeas, garlic, sesame seeds, olive oil, and lemon, is given a southern twist at the Café, where the South's favorite field pea, the black-eyed pea, is swapped in for the traditional chickpea. The result is a deliciously different spread that has a slight crunch of sesame seed and a hint of heat.

CHEF'S NOTE

The spread can be prepared and stored in the refrigerator up to two days before serving.

---

8 garlic cloves, gently cracked, then peeled

2 fresh thyme sprigs

1 teaspoon kosher salt

½ teaspoon freshly ground black pepper

2 tablespoons extra-virgin olive oil

1 pound black-eyed peas, cooked from dry or canned (drained and rinsed)

1½ tablespoons tahini

3 tablespoons freshly squeezed lemon juice

⅛ teaspoon cayenne pepper

4 tablespoons amber peanut oil or extra-virgin olive oil, plus more for drizzling

1 tablespoon toasted benne (sesame) seeds, for garnish

Benne Seed Flatbread Crisps (page 157), for serving

Carrot and celery sticks, for serving

THE NIGHT BEFORE

Sort through the black-eyed peas to remove any debris and stones. Place the beans in a colander and rinse under cold water. Transfer to a large soup pot and cover with cold water. The water level should reach at least 2 inches above the beans. Leave to soak overnight.

THE NEXT DAY

Preheat the oven to 375°F.

Prepare a 6-by-6-inch piece of aluminum foil. Put the garlic cloves, thyme, salt, pepper, and olive oil in the center of the foil. Fold the foil inward from |all four sides to create a tightly sealed parcel. Place on a baking sheet and bake until the garlic is tender, about 35 minutes.

Transfer the baked garlic and olive oil to a food processor (discard the thyme sprigs). Drain and rinse the peas, then transfer to food processor. Add the tahini, lemon juice, and cayenne. Blend until a coarse mixture is formed. Continue blending while adding the peanut oil in a slow, steady stream until a creamy emulsion is formed.

Adjust the seasoning with salt and pepper as needed and transfer to a shallow serving bowl. Garnish with the benne seeds and a drizzle of peanut oil. Serve with Benne Seed Flatbread Crisps and carrot and celery sticks.

PEAS

Few foods are more closely linked with African Americans than the field pea, which is thought to be indigenous to the West African forest-savanna complex. There the peas were planted on the borders of fields to help keep down the weeds and enrich the soil, and cattle grazed on the stems and vines; hence the names "field pea" and "cowpea." Taken to the Americas during the period of the slave trade, they were growing in the Carolina colonies before the early 1700s, became one of the area's first cash crops, and were exported to the Caribbean colonies, where they were also prized.

The black-eyed pea is undoubtedly the best known of the field peas, but there are also crowder peas (named for the way that they "crowd" the pod), pinkeyes (so-called for their distinctive pink "eye"), and the prissily named lady peas. Black-eyed peas have become a symbol of good luck in the United States, first among African Americans and then by extension throughout much of the South, where they are traditionally consumed on New Year's Day, often with rice and ham hock or bacon in Hoppin' John with a side of greens. A strong partisan of this West African native, George Washington Carver not only encouraged farmers to cultivate black-eyed peas to fix nitrogen in the soil but also reminded folks that field peas can "be prepared in a sufficient number of ways to suit the most fastidious palate" and provided more than forty recipes to guide them.

SERVES

4 to 6

ACTIVE TIME
20 MINS
🕐
TOTAL TIME
**4 HRS
20 MINS**

VEGETARIAN

TEXAS
CAVIAR

ALSO KNOWN AS MARINATED black-eyed peas, Texas Caviar is the state's version of a marinated bean salad. It consists of only black-eyed peas or of a mix of various beans, minced bell pepper, and corn. Created around 1940, it has become a Lone Star classic and is guaranteed to turn up at many a Juneteenth celebration.

2½ cups cooked black-eyed peas, preferably from fresh or frozen (rinse and drain well if using canned peas)

1 yellow bell pepper, finely diced

1 cup cilantro leaves, roughly chopped

1 serrano pepper, seeded and finely chopped

1 small jalapeño pepper, seeded and finely chopped

3 plum tomatoes, seeded and diced

6 scallions, white and light green parts, thinly sliced

¼ cup red onion, diced

¼ cup extra-virgin olive oil

¼ cup freshly squeezed lime juice

1 teaspoon garlic, finely chopped

1 teaspoon ground cumin

1 teaspoon kosher salt

Freshly ground black pepper

Hot sauce, for seasoning

In a large bowl, combine all the ingredients and gently mix until well blended. Add the cumin and salt. Adjust the seasoning with black pepper and hot sauce to taste. Transfer to the refrigerator to marinate for a minimum of 4 hours.

Serve as a side salad or with tortilla chips.

MAKES
ABOUT
36
HUSH
PUPPIES

ACTIVE TIME
45 MINS

TOTAL TIME
45 MINS

SWEET ONION & CORN
HUSH PUPPIES
WITH RED PEPPER REMOULADE

ONE LEGEND HAS IT THAT hush puppies originated as balls of dough made by hunters or fishermen for throwing to dogs to quiet them while food was cooking. A second tale says the small balls of fried cornmeal dough were invented during the Civil War by Confederate soldiers as a way to quiet their dogs to avoid detection. Whatever the story, the fried balls are a perfect snack for humans, especially when served with a red pepper remoulade for dipping.

RED PEPPER REMOULADE

1 cup mayonnaise, preferably Duke's

¼ cup Dijon mustard

¼ cup roasted red pepper, chopped into a paste

1 shallot, finely chopped

1½ tablespoons prepared horseradish

1 tablespoon cider vinegar

1 tablespoon fresh flat-leaf parsley, chopped

1 teaspoon freshly squeezed lemon juice

1 teaspoon Tabasco sauce

½ teaspoon smoked paprika

½ teaspoon kosher salt

SWEET ONION & CORN HUSH PUPPIES

2 cups white cornmeal, preferably stone-ground

2 tablespoons all-purpose flour

1 teaspoon kosher salt

1 teaspoon baking powder

1 teaspoon baking soda

1½ cups buttermilk, preferably full fat

1 large egg yolk

¾ cup Vidalia, or other sweet onion, finely grated, (use a box grater)

¼ cup scallion, white and light green parts, thinly sliced

¾ cup fresh or frozen corn kernels, cooked

3 large egg whites, beaten to stiff peaks

2½ cups vegetable oil, for frying

TO MAKE THE RED PEPPER REMOULADE

Combine all the ingredients in a medium bowl, whisking to blend well. Cover and store in the refrigerator for up to 3 days.

TO MAKE THE SWEET ONION & CORN HUSH PUPPIES

Sift the cornmeal, flour, salt, baking powder, and baking soda together into a medium bowl. In a small bowl, mix together the buttermilk and egg yolk. Stir the buttermilk mixture into the dry ingredients. Fold in the onion and scallions, mixing gently until all the ingredients are incorporated. Gently fold in the corn kernels followed by the beaten egg whites. Do not overmix or the egg whites will deflate.

Pour the vegetable oil into a large cast iron skillet and heat to 350°F on a deep-frying thermometer (or use a tabletop deep fryer). Using a soupspoon or small ice cream scoop, carefully drop spoonfuls of batter into the hot oil, 15 to 18 at a time. Fry until the hush puppies are golden brown, 3 to 4 minutes. Remove them from the fryer with a slotted spoon and place on a plate lined with paper towels to drain excess oil. Serve hot with the Red Pepper Remoulade.

AGRICULTURAL
SOUTH

SERVES
6

ACTIVE TIME
15 MINS
🕐
TOTAL TIME
40 MINS

"CRACKLIN'"
CORN BREAD

CRACKLINGS, OR CRACKLIN'S, is the name for pieces of pork skin that have been deep-fried (or occasionally roasted) to a crisp finish. Also known as pork rinds, they impart a smoked bacon flavor and extra crunch when added to corn bread batter. The corn bread is best served fresh from the oven, as the cracklings can get hard as they cool. In this recipe, bacon has been substituted for the traditional cracklings, which can be difficult to source.

CHEF'S NOTE
Artisanal cornmeal and bacon are key to the success of this dish.

5 ounces high-quality hardwood-smoked bacon, chilled in the freezer for 20 minutes

2 cups coarse yellow cornmeal, preferably stone-ground

½ teaspoon baking soda

½ teaspoon baking powder

1½ cups buttermilk, preferably full fat

1 large egg

1 teaspoon fine sea salt

Preheat the oven to 450°F.

Mince the bacon slices into very fine pieces. Transfer to a medium skillet over medium heat and cook to render the fat and crisp the bits. Then pour the bacon bits and fat into a strainer, separately reserving both bits and fat. You will need 6 tablespoons bacon fat total. If you have less, make up the difference for the batter with melted butter.

In a large bowl, whisk together the cornmeal, baking soda, and baking powder.

In a separate bowl, mix together the buttermilk, egg, salt, and 5 tablespoons of the rendered bacon fat.

Put a 9-inch cast iron skillet into the hot oven to heat for 8 minutes.

Using a rubber spatula, gently fold the buttermilk mixture into the dry ingredients, then add the bacon bits and stir just until fully incorporated. Do not overmix.

Remove the hot skillet from the oven and place on the stovetop over high heat. Add the remaining 1 tablespoon bacon fat to the skillet and tilt the skillet until the base is fully coated. Now quickly pour the corn bread batter into the hot skillet and swirl it carefully, evenly distributing it.

Return the skillet to the oven and bake for about 20 minutes. To test doneness, insert a toothpick into the center of the corn bread and quickly remove. If it comes out clean, the bread is done. Serve hot and fresh out of the oven.

JOHNNYCAKES

CONTINENTAL
UNITED STATES

SERVES
4 to **6**

ACTIVE TIME
35 MINS

🕐
TOTAL TIME
35 MINS

THERE ARE MANY KINDS OF johnnycakes, sometimes called journey cakes or hoecakes. In the South and up and down the Atlantic Seaboard, they are often a cornmeal flatbread. Native Americans originated these hearty cakes, and some food historians believe the word *johnnycake* comes from the colonial pronunciation of Shawnee cake.

2 cups white cornmeal, preferably stone-ground

1 teaspoon kosher salt

¼ teaspoon baking powder

½ teaspoon sugar

1 cup water

1 cup whole milk

Unsalted butter and favorite syrup, for serving

Sift the cornmeal, salt, baking powder, and sugar together into a medium bowl.

Combine the water and milk in a small saucepan and bring to a simmer. Once heated, immediately remove from the heat and whisk into the cornmeal mixture, stirring until the batter is smooth.

Grease a large cast iron skillet or hoecake pan with butter or bacon drippings and preheat over medium heat. Spoon the batter onto the hot skillet, forming 3-inch cakes and being careful not to crowd the pan. Cook, turning once, until golden brown, 3 to 4 minutes per side. Transfer to a platter and keep warm. Repeat with the remaining batter, greasing the skillet as needed.

Serve hot with butter and syrup.

SERVES
4 to 8

ACTIVE TIME
20 MINS

TOTAL TIME
35 MINS

HOT WATER
CORN BREAD

HOT WATER CORN BREAD IS a quick way to turn out a batch of corn bread. The simple cornmeal mixture is shaped into cakes, which are then traditionally fried for just minutes in a cast iron skillet.

CHEF'S NOTE

For a lighter corn bread, reduce the amount of cornmeal by ¼ cup and substitute the same amount of all-purpose flour. For a fuller flavor, use bacon drippings for the vegetable oil.

1½ cups cold water

2 cups white cornmeal, preferably stone-ground

2 teaspoons kosher salt

2 tablespoons butter, melted, plus more for serving

3 to 4 tablespoons vegetable oil

Pour the water into a pot and bring to a boil.

Put the cornmeal and salt in a medium bowl. Pour the boiling water over the cornmeal, add the melted butter, and stir well until a batter is formed. Allow the cornmeal to cool until you can comfortably handle it. Then, using your hands, form into patties about 3 inches in diameter and ¾ inch thick.

Pour the vegetable oil into a 10-inch cast iron skillet and heat over medium heat. When the oil is hot, place the corn cakes in the pan and cook until a golden brown crust forms, 2 to 3 minutes. Then flip each corn cake over and cook the other side for 2 to 3 minutes longer, until golden brown.

Transfer to a platter lined with paper towels to drain off excess oil and keep warm. Repeat with the remaining corn cakes.

Serve the corn bread hot with butter.

YELLOW
CORN BREAD

SERVES

6

ACTIVE TIME
10 MINS

TOTAL TIME
40 MINS

CORN IS A NATIVE AMERICAN gift to African American cooking. Here, the two cultures combine with European tradition in this popular southern hot bread. Many a conversation has broken down over whether or not sugar should be added to the batter. At the Café, a bit of sugar is included. Remember, though, it's corn bread, not cake.

½ cup (1 stick) unsalted butter

1½ cups all-purpose flour

1 cup coarse yellow cornmeal, preferably stone-ground

2 teaspoons fine sea salt

2 teaspoons baking powder

¼ teaspoon baking soda

1¼ cups buttermilk, preferably full fat

1 large egg

¼ cup sugar

Preheat the oven to 400°F. Butter a 9-inch cast iron skillet or 8-by-8-inch baking dish.

In a large bowl, whisk together the flour, cornmeal, salt, baking powder, and baking soda.

Melt the butter and let cool slightly. Then, in a medium bowl, whisk the buttermilk, egg, sugar, and melted butter until well blended.

Using a rubber spatula, fold the buttermilk mixture into the dry ingredients and blend together. Do not overmix. Pour the batter into the prepared pan.

Bake for 20 to 25 minutes. To test doneness, insert a toothpick into the center of the corn bread and quickly remove. If it comes out clean, the bread is done. Serve warm.

MAKES
ABOUT
8

ACTIVE TIME
20 MINS

TOTAL TIME
35 MINS

BUTTERMILK
BISCUITS

BISCUITS ARE A STAPLE OF the Southern bread basket. Slathered with butter and sorghum or cane syrup at breakfast or dripping with melted butter at other meals, the best buttermilk biscuits—light, tender, and extra flaky—are the test of a good baker.

CHEF'S NOTE

For a true Southern-style biscuit, use a low-gluten white flour such as White Lily. Lard will provide old-style flavor, but butter can be substituted.

2 cups self-rising white flour

¼ teaspoon kosher salt

4 tablespoons cold lard or butter, cut into small dice

¾ cup buttermilk, plus up to ¼ cup if needed, preferably full fat

2 tablespoons butter, melted

Preheat the oven to 450°F. Line a baking sheet with parchment paper.

In a large bowl, combine the flour and salt. Using a pastry blender or two knives cut the lard into the flour mixture until coarse, pea-sized crumbs form. Moisten the flour mixture with the buttermilk, stirring and lightly tossing, just until the mixture pulls together into a dough. If the dough is too dry, add up to ¼ cup more buttermilk.

Turn the dough out onto a floured surface and knead it four times until smooth, being careful not to overmix. Lightly dust a rolling pin with flour and roll out the dough ¾-inch thick. Dust a 2- to 3-inch round biscuit cutter with flour and cut out rounds from the dough.

Transfer the biscuits to the prepared baking sheet, placing them about ¼ inch apart. (This placement will yield a soft, tender biscuit, as it keeps the biscuits from becoming crispy on the sides.)

Bake for 10 to 12 minutes, until risen and golden brown. Remove from the oven and brush the tops with the melted butter. Serve the biscuits hot.

DROP BISCUITS

MAKES
12
(3-INCH)
BISCUITS

ACTIVE TIME
25 MINS

TOTAL TIME
40 MINS

THESE BISCUITS ARE SO quick and easy—the dough is simply stirred together in a bowl and then dropped onto a baking pan—they are sometimes called "emergency biscuits."

CHEF'S NOTE
For easy cleanup, be sure to line the baking sheet with parchment paper.

4 cups all-purpose flour

2 teaspoons fine sea salt

2 tablespoons baking powder

1 cup (2 sticks) unsalted butter, cut into small dice, plus 4 tablespoons, melted, for brushing

2 cups whole milk

Preheat the oven to 400°F. Line a baking sheet with parchment paper.

Sift the flour, salt, and baking powder into a large mixing bowl. Using a pastry blender or two knives, cut the diced butter into the flour mixture until coarse, pea-sized crumbs form.

With a rubber spatula, fold in the milk and gently mix until fully absorbed and a wet dough has formed.

Using a large kitchen spoon or scoop, distribute the dough into 12 portions on the prepared baking sheet, placing them about ¾ inch apart.

Bake for about 12 minutes, until golden brown. Remove from the oven and brush the tops with the melted butter. Serve the biscuits hot.

SWEET POTATO
BISCUITS

AGRICULTURAL
SOUTH

MAKES
1 doz.

ACTIVE TIME
30 MINS
🕐
TOTAL TIME
1 HR

MASHED SWEET POTATOES and sorghum (or dark maple syrup) add sweetness and texture to these biscuits, an old southern specialty. Thomas Jefferson enjoyed an early version of these biscuits in 1774, when they were served at the First Continental Congress, and perhaps James Hemings, his enslaved chef, made them for him after that.

CHEF'S NOTE

The sweet potatoes should be baked, peeled, and mashed the night before and then refrigerated overnight. Chilling the butter in the freezer makes it easier to work into the dry ingredients.

2¼ cups all-purpose flour

1 tablespoon baking powder

½ teaspoon baking soda

1 teaspoon fine sea salt

1 pinch freshly grated nutmeg

½ teaspoon ground cinnamon

¾ cup mashed sweet potatoes, cold

¼ cup sorghum syrup, molasses, or dark maple syrup

¾ cup full fat buttermilk, plus more for brushing

8 tablespoons (1 stick) unsalted butter, cut into small cubes and chilled in freezer for 15 minutes

---

Preheat the oven to 450°F. Line a baking sheet with parchment paper.

Sift the flour, baking powder, baking soda, salt, nutmeg, and cinnamon into a large bowl.

In a medium bowl, mix the mashed sweet potatoes with the sorghum and buttermilk until smooth and creamy. Set aside.

With a pastry blender or two knives, cut the butter into the flour mixture until fully incorporated and a coarse, mealy consistency forms.

Make a well in the center of the flour–butter mixture. Pour the sweet potato mixture into the well. With a rubber spatula, begin folding it into the dry ingredients. Mix just to the point that a dough forms. Do not overmix.

Turn out the dough on to a floured surface and roll out 1-inch thick. Dust a 2-inch round biscuit cutter with flour (use a 1½- or 2-inch cutter for cocktail-size biscuits), and cut out the biscuits. Transfer them to the prepared baking sheet, spacing them about 1 inch apart.

Brush the tops of the biscuits with buttermilk. Bake for 14 to 18 minutes, until golden brown. Serve the biscuits hot.

CULINARY
COUSINS

MAKES

8

ACTIVE TIME
50 MINS
⏱
TOTAL TIME
**1 HR
50 MINS**

VEGETARIAN

ROTI

ROTI, WHICH COMES FROM the Sanskrit word for bread, is a flatbread from India that harks back to the early days of the Indus Valley civilization, when farmers grew wheat and other grains. It traveled to the Caribbean and South America with indentured Indian servants, and today is especially prized in Trinidad and Tobago and Guyana, where it is not only the name of a favorite local dish but also of the flatbread wrapper that surrounds it.

⅓ cup warm water (100° to 110°F)

¼ teaspoon sugar

1 teaspoon active dry yeast

2 cups all-purpose flour

1 teaspoon ground turmeric

½ teaspoon ground cumin

½ teaspoon salt

½ teaspoon freshly ground black pepper

2 tablespoons butter, divided

In a small bowl, combine the warm water, sugar, and yeast and let rest until the mixture bubbles, about 5 minutes.

In a large bowl, combine the flour, turmeric, cumin, salt, and pepper. Gradually pour the yeast mixture into the flour mixture, stirring with a wooden spoon until a slightly firm dough forms. If the dough is too dry, add a little warm water to bring the dough together.

Knead the dough until smooth and elastic, then transfer back into the bowl and cover with a damp cloth. Set aside in a warm place to rise until doubled in size, about 1 hour.

Divide the dough into eight equal pieces. On a lightly floured surface, roll out each piece into a 6-inch circle.

In a 10-inch sauté pan, melt ¾ teaspoon of the butter over medium-high heat. Add a dough circle and fry, turning once, until golden brown, 2 to 3 minutes per side. Transfer to a plate and keep warm. Repeat with the remaining dough circles and butter.

Serve warm (within 30 minutes of making) and fill with Trini Doubles (page 121).

BENNE SEED
FLATBREAD CRISPS

THIS CRISP, GOLDEN BROWN, wafer-like flatbread, made from a simple mixture of flour, cornmeal, and sesame seeds, is a wonderful addition to any bread basket. It can also double as a chip or crisp for dips and spreads and is good alongside cheese.

1⅓ cups all-purpose flour

1⅓ cups finely milled corn flour

3 tablespoons benne (sesame) seeds

1 teaspoon fine sea salt

¾ cup lukewarm water

2 tablespoons extra-virgin olive oil, plus more for brushing

2 tablespoons kosher salt, divided

In a medium bowl, whisk together the flour, corn flour, benne seeds, and sea salt until well blended. Transfer the mixture to the bowl of a stand mixer with a dough hook attachment. Set the mixer at low speed and turn it on.

Slowly pour the lukewarm water and 2 tablespoons olive oil into the flour mixture and mix until fully absorbed and a dough has formed. With the mixer on its lowest setting, knead the dough for 3 minutes. Remove the dough from the bowl and tightly wrap in plastic wrap. Let rest for 20 minutes.

Preheat the oven to 450°F. Line several baking sheets with parchment paper. If you have half sheet pans, each pan will hold 2 flatbreads.

On a floured work surface, divide the dough into 12 equal pieces and form them into balls. Using a rolling pin, roll out each ball as thinly as possible into an 8-by-4-inch rectangle, being careful there are no holes in the dough.

Transfer 1 or 2 dough rectangles (depending on the size of the pan) to each prepared baking sheet, and brush with olive oil. Lightly sprinkle the surface with the kosher salt. If making several batches, (be sure to let a baking sheet cool completely before placing an unbaked flatbread on it.)

Place a baking sheet in the oven and bake untilthe flatbread is golden brown and crisp, about 4 minutes. Transfer the bread to a wire rack to cool. Repeat until all the flatbreads are baked.

Break the flatbreads into large pieces before serving.

SWEETS
AND
DRINKS

**FRIED APPLE
HAND PIES**

Top left: *Grocery Store, 14th & U Streets*, Washington, DC, ca. 1940. Photograph by Robert H. McNeill.

Top middle: *Peace Meals*, ca. 1937; printed 1981. From the series *Harlem Document*. Photograph by Aaron Siskind.

Opposite, bottom: Two couples seated at a table, 1944.

RED VELVET CAKE

SWEETS
AND
DRINKS

Feature: Northern States / 162

Basic Pie Crust / 164

Chocolate Chess Pie / 165

Sweet Potato Pie / 167

Bourbon Pecan Pie / 169

Lemon Meringue Pie / 170

Lemon Curd Blueberry Tart / 171

Fried Apple Hand Pies / 172

High Mesa Peach & Blackberry Cobbler / 175

Buttermilk Tea Cakes / 176

Molasses Rum Raisin Cake / 177

Joe Froggers / 178

Lemon-Glazed Pound Cake / 180

Charleston Pecan Chewies / 181

Red Velvet Cake / 182

Banana Pudding / 185

Peanut Brittle / 186

Pralines / 188

Hibiscus & Ginger Sweet Tea / 189

Sparkling Watermelon
& Lemon Verbena / 189

Sweet Cherry Lemonade / 191

NORTHERN STATES

The Northern States region, which includes not only the "mythic" North of the enslaved but also the North of the Great Migration, stretches from the Eastern Seaboard to Chicago and parts of the Midwest. Some of its African American neighborhoods date to colonial times, others were settled during the migrations of the nineteenth and twentieth centuries, and still others are of more recent vintage.

From colonial times onward, African Americans in the North have used food service as a vehicle for upward mobility. In 1736, the year of his emancipation, Emmanuel "Manna" Bernoon, a free black in Providence, Rhode Island, opened an oyster and alehouse, that city's first. Bernoon's connection with oysters is not surprising, as African American oystermen were notable throughout the coastal regions. New York's Thomas Downing, for example, earned a fortune with his knowledge of aquaculture (see page 84).

Anne Hampton Northup, the wife of Solomon Northup of *Twelve Years a Slave* fame, worked as a cook at the United States Hotel in Saratoga Springs, New York, and garnered high praise for her culinary skills. In 1853, the same town may have given the world the potato chip when George Crum, an African American chef, produced chips more thinly sliced and crispier than the British game chip.

African American waiters and butlers for hire were the standard in early-nineteenth-century Philadelphia. The catering companies they established rose to such great prominence that historian W. E. B. DuBois called them "as remarkable a trade guild as ever ruled in a mediaeval city."

In the era before supermarkets, northern food hawkers kept their patrons well served with delicacies. African American women in Philadelphia sold a local version of gumbo, a spicy pepper pot stew. In Baltimore, street vendors called arabbers, many of whom were African American, peddled fruits and vegetables from horse-drawn wagons even into the twenty-first century.

The first known African American cookbook also comes from this region. In 1866, Malinda Russell, a free woman of color, published *A Domestic Cook Book: Containing a Careful Selection of Useful Receipts for the Kitchen* in Paw Paw, Michigan, a work that reflects both the tenacity and the culinary inventiveness of African Americans in the Northern States.

JOE FROGGERS

THOMAS DOWNING'S NYC OYSTER PAN ROAST

Top: Egg carton from Muslim Farms, 1968.

Middle: *Pushcart Market,* 1930s. Brownsville, Brooklyn, New York. Photograph by Joe Schwartz.

Bottom: *The Mother's Counsel of True Light Church Baptist enjoys the repast after the Annual Woman's Day program, Chicago, Illinois,* 2005. Photograph by Jason Miccolo Johnson.

CONTINENTAL
UNITED STATES

MAKES

1

**(9-INCH PIE
CRUST)**

ACTIVE TIME
20 MINS

TOTAL TIME
**1 HR
30 MINS**

BASIC PIE CRUST

THE TEST OF A GOOD PIE IS a light, tender, flaky crust. To guarantee that result, use pastry flour and make sure your work surface and the dough is as cold as possible when you are rolling it out. Also, when making the dough, chill the water with ice cubes so the dough stays cold as you mix it.

1 cup pastry flour

½ teaspoon fine sea salt

½ cup cold unsalted butter, cut into ¼-inch cubes

2 tablespoons ice water

Sift the flour and salt into a large bowl. Using a pastry blender or two knives, cut the butter into the flour until the mixture is the consistency of pea-sized crumbs. Slowly add the cold water 1 teaspoon at a time, mixing just until a lightly moist dough is formed. The amount of water needed can vary; it can be more or less than the full amount.

Divide the dough in half and form into two balls. Tightly wrap each ball in plastic wrap and place in the refrigerator until needed. The dough should rest for at least 1 hour.

When ready to use, remove the dough from the refrigerator, allow to rest for 10 minutes, and unwrap. On a lightly floured surface, roll out the dough as directed in individual recipes. For the best results, always work with cold dough.

TO BLIND BAKE A PIE OR TART CRUST

Line the pie dish or tart pan with dough and refrigerate as directed in individual recipes. Preheat the oven to 325°F. Using a fork, prick the base of the pastry shell evenly across its surface about 25 times. Line the shell with a 12-inch round of parchment paper and fill with about 2 cups dried beans (the weight of the beans prevents the dough from puffing up in the oven).

Place the pie dish or tart pan on a baking sheet and bake the crust until lightly golden and fully set, 15 to 20 minutes, carefully lifting the edge of the parchment to check the progress. Transfer to a wire rack, remove the beans and parchment, and let cool completely. (Save the beans for blind baking future crusts.)

CHOCOLATE
CHESS PIE

MAKES

1

9-INCH PIE

ACTIVE TIME
15 MINS

🕐
TOTAL TIME
3 HRS

CHESS PIES, WHICH PROBABLY originated in England, first became a tradition in Virginia, spreading from there to the rest of the South. The classic chess pie has a sweet egg-rich custard filling, with cornmeal (or flour) added to give it its distinctive texture. The custard can also be flavored, typically with lemon, chocolate, or coconut.

1 (9-inch) Basic Pie Crust (opposite page)

1½ cups sugar

4 tablespoons unsalted butter, melted

¼ cup unsweetened cocoa powder

1 teaspoon pure vanilla extract, preferably Bourbon vanilla

2 large eggs

½ cup evaporated milk

1 pinch kosher salt

Whipped cream, for serving

Roll out the dough on a floured surface to a thickness of about ⅜ inch. Line a 9-inch pie dish with the dough, bringing it fully up the sides. Trim off any excess dough and crimp the edge. Place the pie dish in the refrigerator to allow the dough to firm up.

Preheat the oven to 350°F.

In a medium bowl, combine the sugar, melted butter, cocoa, vanilla, eggs, evaporated milk, and salt. Whisk thoroughly until all the ingredients are well blended.

Pour the batter into the pie crust and bake for 35 minutes, until set. Remove from the oven and place on a wire rack to cool completely.

Serve with whipped cream.

SWEET POTATO PIE

AGRICULTURAL
SOUTH

MAKES

1

9-INCH PIE

ACTIVE TIME
30 MINS
🕐

TOTAL TIME
4 HRS

IF IT IS THANKSGIVING IN an African American household, the pie at the center of the dessert spread is more likely made from sweet potato than pumpkin. This connection to sweet potatoes probably goes back to a time when the tubers were the only sweet treat available to many Southerners.

Basic Pie Crust (page 164)

3 medium sweet potatoes (about 1½ pounds)

½ cup (1 stick) unsalted butter, at room temperature

1¼ cups sugar

1 teaspoon ground cinnamon

½ teaspoon freshly grated nutmeg

¼ teaspoon ground allspice

2 teaspoons finely grated lemon zest

1 pinch kosher salt

2 large eggs

1 teaspoon Bourbon vanilla extract

1 tablespoon freshly squeezed lemon juice

Whipped cream, for serving

Put the sweet potatoes in a medium saucepan, cover with water, and bring to a boil over high heat. Boil until fork-tender, about 25 minutes. Drain and let cool to room temperature.

Roll out the dough on a floured surface to a thickness of about ⅜ inch. Line a 9-inch pie dish with the dough, bringing it fully up the sides. Trim off any excess dough and crimp the edge. Place the pie dish in the refrigerator to allow the dough to firm up.

Preheat the oven to 375°F.

When the sweet potatoes have cooled, peel them and place the flesh in the bowl of a stand mixer. Using the paddle attachment, beat the potatoes until smooth. Next pass the mashed sweet potatoes through a strainer to remove any stringy fibers. Reserve the potatoes. Wipe the bowl and paddle clean and return to the mixer.

Add the butter and sugar to the mixer bowl and cream on medium speed, until light and fluffy, about 2 minutes. Add the cinnamon, nutmeg, allspice, lemon zest, and salt. Mix for another 30 seconds. Then, with the mixer speed set to low, add one egg at a time along with the vanilla extract and lemon juice, beating until fully incorporated. Finally, add the pureed sweet potatoes and mix for 1 minute longer.

Pour the sweet potato mixture into the pie crust. Bake for 40 to 60 minutes, until set. To check for doneness, insert a clean toothpick into the center of the pie and quickly remove it; if it comes out clean, the pie is done. Remove from oven and place on a wire rack to cool completely.

Serve with whipped cream.

BOURBON
PECAN PIE

AGRICULTURAL
SOUTH

MAKES

1

9-INCH PIE

ACTIVE TIME
30 MINS
🕐
TOTAL TIME
3 HRS

THE PECAN TREE, WHICH takes its name from an Algonquin word, is native to the American South. Bourbon, distilled from corn, especially in Bourbon County, Kentucky, is the South's favorite brown liquor. Here, this prized American nut is paired with America's most celebrated homegrown spirit to produce a dessert that is 100 percent southern and 100 percent delicious.

CHEF'S NOTE

For best results, use only pure vanilla extract and the best aged bourbon.

Basic Pie Crust (page 164)

1¼ cups packed light brown sugar

¾ cup light corn syrup

4 tablespoons unsalted butter

5 tablespoons aged Kentucky bourbon

½ teaspoon fine sea salt

3 large eggs

1 tablespoon pure vanilla extract, preferably Bourbon vanilla

Scant 2 cups jumbo pecan halves (about 7 ounces)

Whipped cream or vanilla ice cream, for serving

Roll out the dough on a floured surface to a thickness of about ⅜ inch. Line a 9-inch pie dish with the dough, bringing it fully up the sides. Trim off any excess dough and crimp the edge. Place the pie dish in the refrigerator to allow the dough to firm up.

Preheat the oven to 325°F.

Combine the sugar, corn syrup, butter, bourbon, and salt in a saucepan and bring to a boil over medium heat, stirring to dissolve the sugar. Reduce to a simmer and cook for 2 minutes. Remove from the heat and let the mixture cool to lukewarm.

In a medium bowl, whisk the eggs and vanilla together and then add the cooled bourbon syrup mixture. Continue whisking until fully incorporated.

Place the pecans in a single layer on a baking sheet lined with parchment paper and bake for 5 minutes. Be careful not to let them burn. This will give the pecans a toasted flavor. Allow to cool.

Raise the oven temperature to 375°F. Remove the pie dish from the refrigerator and fill it with the cooled pecans. Pour over the bourbon syrup mixture, completely covering the pecans.

Bake for 10 minutes, reduce the temperature to 325°F, and continue to bake for about 40 minutes, until set. Remove from the oven and place on a wire rack to cool completely.

Serve each slice with whipped cream or a scoop of ice cream.

MAKES
1
9-INCH PIE

ACTIVE TIME
20 MINS

TOTAL TIME
**10HRS
30 MINS**

LEMON
MERINGUE PIE

THE TART TASTE OF LEMONS has been featured in desserts since medieval times. In the South, making lemon curd, lemon chess pie, lemon pound cake, lemon bars, and more is common. Here, the versatile citrus fruit turns up in a tart yet sweet lemon meringue pie.

CHEF'S NOTE
Meringue is sensitive to weather and should be prepared only on low-humidity days to keep it from "weeping."

Basic Pie Crust (page 164)

FILLING

1¼ cups sugar

½ teaspoon kosher salt

1½ cups water, divided

1 tablespoon plus ¾ teaspoon finely grated lemon zest

⅓ cup cornstarch

4 large egg yolks

6 tablespoons unsalted butter

½ cup freshly squeezed lemon juice, preferably from Meyer lemons

MERINGUE

3 large egg whites

½ teaspoon Bourbon vanilla extract

1 pinch kosher salt

¼ cup sugar

⅛ teaspoon cream of tartar

TO MAKE THE CRUST
Roll out the dough on a floured surface to a thickness of about ⅜ inch. Line a 9-inch pie dish with the dough, bringing it fully up the sides. Trim off any excess dough and crimp the edge. Place the pie dish in the refrigerator for 30 minutes to firm up the dough, then blind bake the crust as directed on page 164.

TO MAKE THE FILLING
In a medium saucepan, combine the sugar, salt, 1 cup of the water, and lemon zest and bring to a boil, stirring to dissolve the sugar. In a small bowl, whisk together the remaining ½ cup water and the cornstarch until dissolved. Add the cornstarch mixture to the boiling sugar mixture and whisk until thickened. Remove from the heat. In a medium bowl, whisk the egg yolks until blended. Slowly add about ½ cup of the hot mixture while whisking constantly. Then pour into the saucepan. Cook for 1 minute on low heat, stirring constantly. Remove from the heat, and whisk in the butter and lemon juice until smooth. Pour the filling into the prebaked pie crust and let cool.

TO MAKE THE MERINGUE
Preheat the oven to 375°F.

Use an electric mixer to whip the egg whites, vanilla, salt, sugar, and cream of tartar until stiff, firm peaks have formed. Spoon the meringue into a pastry bag fitted with a star tip and pipe generously onto the cooled filling.

Bake the pie for 8 to 10 minutes, until the meringue has set and is golden. Let cool completely on a wire rack, then chill in the refrigerator for 6 to 8 hours before serving.

LEMON CURD
BLUEBERRY TART

MAKES

1

9-INCH
TART

ACTIVE TIME
10 MINS

TOTAL TIME
5 HRS

IN NEW ORLEANS AND OTHER parts of the South, where citrus trees are commonly grown in backyards, cooks faced with a bumper crop of lemons begin to make batches of lemon curd. The curd can be used as a spread on cakes or cupcakes, or it can be mixed with other ingredients, such as the blueberries in this lovely tart.

Basic Pie Crust (page 164)

4 large eggs

1½ cups sugar

⅓ cup heavy cream

1½ tablespoons finely grated lemon zest

1 pinch kosher salt

1 cup freshly squeezed lemon juice, preferably from Meyer lemons

1 pound blueberries

Roll out the dough on a floured surface to a thickness of about ⅜ inch. Line a 9-inch tart pan with a removable bottom with the dough, bringing it fully up the sides and trimming off the excess flush with the rim. Place the tart pan in the refrigerator for 30 minutes to firm up the dough, then blind bake the crust as directed on page 164.

Preheat the oven to 350°F.

In a mixing bowl, whisk the eggs, sugar, cream, lemon zest, salt, and lemon juice until well blended.

Arrange the blueberries in an even layer in the prebaked pie crust. Pour the lemon-egg mixture over the berries to fill the crust.

Bake for 25 minutes, until set. Remove from the oven, transfer to a wire rack to cool, then chill in the refrigerator for 3 to 4 hours before serving. To unmold the tart, place the tart pan on an overturned bowl or glass and gently slide the pan ring downward. Using a wide spatula, carefully slide the tart off the pan bottom onto a serving plate.

CONTINENTAL UNITED STATES

MAKES **10**

ACTIVE TIME **40 MINS**

TOTAL TIME **1 HR 20 MINS**

FRIED APPLE

HAND PIES

A FRIED HAND PIE, OR SWEET turnover, is a traditional grab-'em-and-go food that is perfect for school lunches or summer picnics

CHEF'S NOTE

For a more flavorful pie crust, substitute lard for the vegetable shortening. Frying the pies in peanut oil will also enhance their flavor. The Café makes an apple filling, but any fruit pie filling can be used.

APPLE FILLING

- 3 tablespoons unsalted butter
- 6 apples, peeled, cored, and sliced
- ⅓ cup granulated sugar
- 1½ teaspoons ground cinnamon
- ¼ teaspoon freshly grated nutmeg
- ¼ teaspoon sea salt
- ⅛ teaspoon ground allspice
- 1 pinch ground cloves
- ¼ cup golden raisins
- 2 tablespoons all-purpose flour
- 1½ teaspoons Bourbon vanilla extract

DOUGH

- 2 cups all-purpose flour
- 1 teaspoon baking soda
- ½ teaspoon salt
- 1 teaspoon granulated sugar
- ½ cup vegetable shortening or lard
- 2 tablespoons ice water, plus more if needed
- 4 cups peanut oil or vegetable oil

- ½ cup confectioners' sugar

TO MAKE THE APPLE FILLING

In a large sauté pan over medium heat, melt the butter and cook the apples with the sugar, cinnamon, nutmeg, salt, allspice, and cloves for 2 to 3 minutes.

Next add the raisins, flour, and vanilla and mix well until the apple slices are evenly coated. Reduce the heat and cook for 2 minutes longer, until the apples are soft. Remove from the heat, transfer to a bowl, and refrigerate until fully cooled.

TO MAKE THE DOUGH

Sift the flour and baking soda into a large bowl. Mix in the salt and sugar. Using a pastry blender or two knives, cut the shortening into the flour mixture until the mixture is the consistency of coarse pea-sized crumbs.

Add the ice water to the flour mixture and mix just until the dough begins to hold together (add more water if needed). Be careful not to overmix. Shape the dough into a ball, wrap in plastic wrap, and refrigerate for 30 minutes.

TO MAKE THE HAND PIES

On a lightly floured surface, roll out the dough ¼-inch thick. Using a pastry cutter about 4 inches in diameter, cut out 10 circles.

Place about 3 tablespoons of the apple filling onto one-half of each pastry circle. Moisten the edges of the pastry lightly with water and fold the other half of the pastry over the filling. Press the edges of the dough together firmly to seal. Dip the tines of a fork in flour and press gently along the sealed side of the pie to create a crimped edge.

In a heavy-bottomed stockpot or deep cast iron skillet, heat the oil until it reads 350°F on a deep-frying thermometer. Working in batches to avoid crowding, add the pies to the hot oil and fry until crisp and golden brown, 3 to 4 minutes.

While the pies are frying, prepare a baking sheet lined with several layers of paper towels.

Using a slotted spoon, remove the pies from the oil and transfer to the prepared baking sheet. Allow to cool for a few minutes and then generously dust with the confectioners' sugar. Repeat with the remaining pies. Serve hot or at room temperature.

HIGH MESA PEACH
& BLACKBERRY COBBLER

WESTERN
RANGE

SERVES
4 to **6**

ACTIVE TIME
10 MINS

🕐

TOTAL TIME
**1 HR
30 MINS**

IN MOST PARTS OF THE COUNTRY, a cobbler is a deep-dish fruit dessert topped with a thick drop biscuit or batter crust. In the South, however, a cobbler will sometimes have both a top and bottom crust. Cobbler fillings are usually soupier than pie fillings, with a dense, rich consistency.

CHEF'S NOTE

At the Café, the cobbler has a mixed-fruit filling and only a top crust, which is made from a batter and baked until golden.

8 tablespoons (1 stick) unsalted butter, divided

1 cup sugar

1 teaspoon pure vanilla extract, preferably Bourbon vanilla

1 cup whole milk

1 cup self-rising pastry flour

6 large peaches, peeled, pitted, and sliced

1½ cups blackberries

1 tablespoon freshly squeezed lemon juice

½ teaspoon finely grated lemon zest

Vanilla ice cream, for serving

Preheat the oven to 350°F.

Lightly grease the bottom and sides of a 9-by-13-inch cobbler dish or a 10-inch cast iron skillet with 1 tablespoon of the butter.

Melt the remaining 7 tablespoons butter, pour into a medium bowl, and let cool. Add the sugar, vanilla, milk, and flour and stir to form a batter.

In a large bowl, toss the peaches and blackberries with the lemon juice and zest, mixing evenly. Transfer to the prepared cobbler dish in an even layer.

Pour the batter evenly on top and bake for 45 to 50 minutes, until the cobbler crust is golden brown.

Serve warm with vanilla ice cream.

MAKES
3 doz.
(2-INCH)
TEA CAKES

ACTIVE TIME
15 MINS

TOTAL TIME
**1 HR
20 MINS**

BUTTERMILK
TEA CAKES

ALTHOUGH THEY ARE CALLED cakes, tea cakes are more like shortbread or sugar cookies. For African Americans, they were a special treat and often came with wonderful memories. Perhaps such remembrances are why Harlem renaissance author Zora Neale Hurston, in her novel *Their Eyes Were Watching God*, named the life-affirming character Tea Cake.

4 cups all-purpose flour

2 teaspoons baking powder

1 teaspoon baking soda

1 cup (2 sticks) unsalted butter, at room temperature

2 cups sugar, plus more for sprinkling

2 large eggs, beaten

½ cup full fat buttermilk

1½ teaspoons fine sea salt

2 teaspoons finely grated lemon zest

Sift the flour, baking powder, and baking soda into a large bowl. Set aside.

Using an electric mixer on low speed, cream the butter and sugar, about 4 to 5 minutes. Add the eggs and mix until blended, then add the buttermilk, salt, and lemon zest.

Next add the flour 1 cup at a time to the creamed mixture, beating after each addition just until incorporated. Do not overmix. (The dough will be somewhat stiff at this point.) Remove the dough from the bowl and divide in half. Wrap each piece in plastic wrap and refrigerate for 20 minutes.

Preheat the oven to 375°F. Line a baking sheet with parchment paper.

Lightly dust a work surface with flour. With a rolling pin, roll out half the dough ¼ inch thick. Using a 2-inch cookie cutter or overturned Mason jar or juice glass, cut out circles. Transfer the dough circles to the prepared baking sheet, arranging them ½ inch apart. Lightly sprinkle the tops with sugar. Repeat with the remaining dough.

Bake for 8 to 10 minutes, until the cakes are light golden. Transfer the cakes to a wire rack to cool completely. Store the cakes in an airtight container at room temperature for 2 to 3 days.

MOLASSES
RUM RAISIN CAKE

MAKES
1
9-INCH
CAKE

ACTIVE TIME
20 MINS
🕐
TOTAL TIME
1 DAY
PLUS
OVERNIGHT
SOAKING

THIS CAKE MAKES USE OF molasses, a sugarcane by-product, and of the liquor that is often distilled from it. That pairing is a reminder that sugarcane plantations were common in both southern Louisiana and Florida and in the Caribbean and that African Americans in the hemisphere were inextricably linked to sugar cultivation.

¼ cup raisins

1 tablespoon candied ginger, finely chopped

¼ cup dark rum

1 cup all-purpose flour

¼ teaspoon ground ginger

¼ teaspoon ground cinnamon

⅛ teaspoon salt

1 teaspoon baking soda

4 tablespoons butter

¼ cup packed light brown sugar

½ cup unsulfured molasses

1 large egg

½ cup warm water

Whipped cream, for serving

THE NIGHT BEFORE

Combine the raisins, candied ginger, and rum in a small bowl and soak overnight.

THE NEXT DAY

Preheat the oven to 350°F. Spray a 9-inch round cake pan with vegetable-oil cooking spray and dust with flour.

Sift the flour, ground ginger, cinnamon, salt, and baking soda together into a medium bowl.

Using a stand mixer with the paddle attachment, cream the butter and brown sugar together on low speed for 4 minutes. Add the molasses and egg and mix for another 2 minutes. Then add the water and mix for 1 minute longer.

Now add the spiced flour mixture and beat just until a batter forms. With a spatula, gently fold in the rum-raisin mixture.

Pour the batter into the prepared pan and bake for 20 to 25 minutes, until set. Transfer to a wire rack and cool to room temperature. Serve with whipped cream.

NORTHERN
STATES

MAKES

2 doz.
COOKIES

ACTIVE TIME
30 MINS

TOTAL TIME
3 HRS

JOE FROGGERS

THESE MOLASSES-SPICE cookies are named for Joe Brown, an African American who lived in Marblehead, Massachusetts, and who was thought to have been born enslaved and gained his freedom through military service in the Revolutionary War. He purchased a tavern with his wife, Lucretia, where they developed the recipe for the cookies. Originally prepared with rum and seawater, they were long lasting and became one of the standard provisions on clipper ships.

CHEF'S NOTE

These molasses cookies are easy to make. The originals were the size of lily pads, but they can be made in any size and shape. For the best flavor, be sure to use spices that have not been on your cupboard shelf too long.

⅓ cup water

1 cup molasses

2½ tablespoons aged dark rum

3½ cups all-purpose flour

1½ teaspoons fine sea salt

1 teaspoon baking soda

1¼ teaspoons ground ginger

½ teaspoon ground cloves

½ teaspoon ground allspice

¼ teaspoon freshly grated nutmeg

½ cup (1 stick) butter, at room temperature

1 cup sugar, plus more for sprinkling

Combine the water, molasses, and rum in a small saucepan, bring to a simmer, and simmer for 1 minute. Remove from the heat and let cool.

Sift the flour, salt, baking soda, ginger, cloves, allspice, and nutmeg together into a bowl.

Using a stand mixer with the paddle attachment, cream the butter and and sugar together on medium-low speed until light and fluffy, about 3 minutes. Add the cooled molasses-rum mixture and beat until blended.

Reduce the mixer speed to low and gradually add the dry ingredients. Mix just until all the ingredients are incorporated and a dough forms (less than 1 minute). Do not overmix.

Divide the dough in half and wrap each piece in plastic wrap. Chill in the refrigerator for 1 hour.

Preheat the oven to 375°F. Line 2 baking sheets with parchment paper.

Using a large spring-action ice cream scoop, place scoops of dough on the prepared baking sheets, spacing them about 1 inch apart. Sprinkle the tops with sugar.

Bake until the cookies are set but still chewy, 6 to 8 minutes.

Let the cookies cool to room temperature. Transfer to an airtight container and store at room temperature. These cookies dry out quickly, so they should be consumed within 24 hours.

CONTINENTAL
UNITED STATES

—

MAKES

2

(9-BY-5-INCH)
LOAVES

—

ACTIVE TIME
25 MINS

⏱

TOTAL TIME
3 HRS

LEMON-GLAZED
POUND CAKE

THE POUND CAKE WAS SO named because it called for one pound of each of four ingredients; sugar, butter, flour, and eggs. Traditionally baked in a loaf pan, it has a dense crumb and a rich flavor and can be served plain or topped with ice cream, fresh fruit, preserved fruit, or jam.

LEMON GLAZE

2 cups confectioners' sugar

4 tablespoons freshly squeezed lemon juice

CAKE

3¼ cups all-purpose flour

1 tablespoon baking powder

2 teaspoons fine sea salt

2 cups (4 sticks) unsalted butter, preferably high-fat European style, at room temperature

2¼ cups sugar

1 teaspoon pure lemon extract

2 teaspoons finely grated lemon zest

9 large eggs

TO MAKE THE LEMON GLAZE

Whisk the confectioners' sugar into the lemon juice in a small bowl until a silky, syrup-like consistency has been achieved. Cover tightly with plastic wrap and reserve.

TO MAKE THE CAKE

Preheat the oven to 325°F. Lightly butter and flour two 9-by-5-inch loaf pans.

Sift the flour, baking powder, and salt into a large bowl and set aside.

Using a stand mixer with the paddle attachment, cream the butter and sugar together on high speed for 9 minutes. Throughout the creaming process, scrape the sides of the bowl to ensure thorough blending. The mixture should be light, fluffy, and silky.

Reduce the speed to medium and add the lemon extract and zest, followed by one egg at a time, beating after each addition until fully incorporated.

Add the flour in two batches, mixing after each addition just until incorporated. Do not overmix.

Divide the batter between the prepared loaf pans and tap each pan on the work surface to remove any air bubbles. With a spatula, smooth and level the batter. Bake for 60 to 70 minutes. The cake is done when a skewer inserted into the center of a loaf and removed quickly comes out clean.

Transfer the loaf pans to a wire rack and let cool for 25 minutes. Then turn the cakes out onto the rack and let cool completely.

Drizzle the tops of the cooled cakes generously with the lemon glaze. Allow the glaze to dry for about 1 hour before serving.

CHARLESTON
PECAN CHEWIES

AGRICULTURAL
SOUTH

MAKES
48
CHEWIES

ACTIVE TIME
30 MINS
🕐

TOTAL TIME
**1 HR
45 MINS**

HOMEMADE SWEETS WERE the only treats available for many in the days when the local store was miles away and transport, public or private, was limited. This brownie-like confection is rich with vanilla flavor and dense with the crunch of pecan bits.

CHEF'S NOTE

Be careful not to overcook these sweets, and when storing them, wrap them tightly in plastic wrap to preserve their chewy freshness.

1 cup unsalted butter, melted

1 cup packed dark brown sugar

1 cup granulated sugar

2 large eggs

1 tablespoon pure vanilla extract, preferably Bourbon vanilla

2 cups all-purpose flour

1 tablespoon baking powder

1 teaspoon fine sea salt

2 cups pecan halves
(about 7 ounces), chopped

Preheat the oven to 300°F. Line a 9-by-13-inch baking sheet with parchment paper and coat with vegetable-oil cooking spray.

Using a stand mixer with the paddle attachment, beat the butter, brown sugar, and granulated sugar together on low speed until a creamy, silky texture. Beat in the eggs one at a time, beating after each addition until fully incorporated, and then beat in the vanilla.

Gradually add the flour, baking powder, and salt, beating just until incorporated. Do not overmix. Using a spatula, gently fold in the pecans.

Evenly spread the batter onto the prepared baking sheet. Bake for about 35 minutes, until set and lightly golden. Let cool completely on a wire rack, then cut into 2-inch squares.

Store the chewies tightly wrapped in plastic wrap or in an airtight container to prevent them from drying out. They will keep for 1 day.

MAKES
1
2-INCH
LAYER
CAKE

ACTIVE TIME
45 MINS

TOTAL TIME
**3 HRS
15 MINS**

RED VELVET
CAKE

ALTHOUGH MANY THINK that red velvet cake has been an American standby for centuries, it is actually a twentieth-century invention, having originated in the 1920s. The ruby-hued chocolate cake was later adopted with delight by African Americans and began turning up on their menus. The famous Amy Ruth's soul food restaurant in Harlem began serving it in 1998, and Cake Man Raven opened one of the first bakeries devoted to the cake in Brooklyn in 2000.

CAKE

2½ cups cake flour

2 tablespoons Dutch-process cocoa powder

1 teaspoon baking soda

½ teaspoon fine sea salt

1½ cups vegetable oil

2 large eggs

1½ cups granulated sugar

1 cup buttermilk, preferably full fat

2 tablespoons red food coloring

1 teaspoon pure vanilla extract, preferably Bourbon vanilla

1 teaspoon distilled white vinegar

FROSTING

½ pound (2½ sticks) unsalted butter, at room temperature

4 cups confectioners' sugar, sifted

1 teaspoon Bourbon vanilla extract

1 pound cream cheese, at room temperature

¼ cup mascarpone cheese

½ cup pecans, finely chopped

TO MAKE THE CAKE

Preheat the oven to 350°F. Butter and lightly flour two 8-by-3-inch nonstick cake pans.

In a medium bowl, whisk together the flour, cocoa, baking soda, and salt.

Combine the oil, eggs, sugar, buttermilk, food coloring, vanilla, and vinegar in the bowl of a stand mixer. Using the whisk attachment, mix on medium-low speed until the mixture is smooth.

Set the mixer at low speed and gradually add the dry ingredients, mixing just to the point a batter has formed. Stop the machine, scrape down the sides of the bowl, and then mix for another 30 seconds.

Evenly divide the batter between the prepared cake pans. Bake until the cake pulls away slightly from the sides of the pans, about 30 minutes. A toothpick inserted in the center should come out clean. Invert the cakes onto wire racks, lift off the pan, turn upright, and let cool to room temperature.

TO MAKE THE FROSTING

Combine the butter, sugar, and vanilla in the bowl of the stand mixer. With the paddle attachment, mix the ingredients on medium speed until they are smooth and creamy. Add the cream cheese and mascarpone and mix until well blended.

TO ASSEMBLE THE CAKE

Using a long serrated knife, shave off a very thin layer of cake from the top and bottom of each cake layer (this will help the frosting cling to the cake). Place the trimmings in the bowl of a food processor and process to very fine crumbs; reserve for the decoration.

Set one of the cake layers on a cake stand. With a narrow offset spatula, spread a layer of frosting across the top of the first layer, spreading it to an even depth of ½ inch. Place the second cake layer on top. With the remaining frosting, evenly cover the sides and top of the cake.

Mix together the reserved cake crumbs and pecans. Immediately after applying frosting, decorate the sides of the cake with a thin layer of the crumb mixture. The top of the cake should remain frosted white. Store the cake in the refrigerator for up to 2 days.

BANANA PUDDING

✤

AGRICULTURAL
SOUTH

SERVES
6

ACTIVE TIME
45 MINS
⊙
TOTAL TIME
**1 HR
45 MINS**

BANANAS WERE A RARE TREAT in the United States in the years before the Civil War. But by the end of the 1870s, they were becoming more widely available, with most of them arriving at the port of New Orleans. Banana pudding soon became a popular menu item, though it was not the same banana pudding we know and love today. That's because there were no vanilla wafers in the mix. Then, in the 1940s, Nabisco printed a recipe for banana pudding on its vanilla wafer box that gradually became the standard southern classic.

CHEF'S NOTE

Use champagne coupes or Collins glasses for more formal individual servings.

1 vanilla bean, split, seeds scraped out

1½ teaspoons bourbon

3 cups half-and-half

3 large eggs

¾ cup superfine sugar, plus 1 teaspoon

2 tablespoons cornstarch

4 large ripe bananas

1 tablespoon freshly squeezed lemon juice

42 vanilla wafers

1 cup whipped cream

6 fresh mint sprigs

In a small bowl, mix the vanilla pulp scraped from the pod with the bourbon.

In a medium saucepan, mix the half-and-half with the vanilla-bourbon blend and heat to a low simmer. While the cream is heating, whisk the eggs, the ¾ cup sugar, and the cornstarch in a medium stainless steel bowl until well blended and smooth.

Slowly pour the hot cream into the egg mixture while whisking constantly until fully incorporated. Return the mixture to the saucepan and stir over low heat until it thickens, about 3 minutes. It is critical to stir the whole time to avoid curdling. Remove from the heat, transfer to a bowl, and allow to cool to room temperature. Cover with plastic wrap, pressing it directly on the surface of the pudding to prevent a skin from forming, and refrigerate for 1 hour.

While the custard cools, peel the bananas, cut into ½-inch-thick rounds, and place in a medium bowl. In a small bowl, mix the lemon juice with the remaining 1 teaspoon sugar, then toss with the bananas to prevent oxidation.

Once the custard is cold, remove it from the refrigerator. Place 1 well-rounded spoonful of custard on the bottom of each individual serving dish. Follow this with 4 or 5 slices of banana, then 2 or 3 vanilla wafers. Repeat this layering until the glass is full (leaving a ½-inch headspace at the top). Garnish each glass with a generous dollop of whipped cream, a fresh mint sprig, and a vanilla wafer.

MAKES
4½ lbs.

ACTIVE TIME
1 HR

TOTAL TIME
3 HRS

CLASSIC
PEANUT BRITTLE

NO ONE KNOWS THE EXACT origin of peanut brittle, but most agree that the American version of the hard sugar candy embedded with peanuts is southern in origin. One of the most popular tales attributes its creation to a cook who, while making taffy, mistakenly dumped in baking soda instead of cream of tartar, which yielded a hard, crunchy brittle rather than a soft, chewy taffy.

CHEF'S NOTE
This brittle will keep in an airtight container at room temperature for up to 2 weeks. Other nuts, like cashews or pecans, can be substituted for the peanuts.

2 cups sugar

1 cup light corn syrup

½ cup cold water

4 tablespoons unsalted butter

2¾ cups shelled Virginia unsalted peanuts, split

1½ teaspoons baking soda

2 or 3 pinches sea salt

Line two large baking sheets with nonstick silicone mats or parchment paper sprayed with vegetable-oil cooking spray.

Lightly coat the sides of a large, deep saucepan with cooking spray. Combine the sugar, corn syrup, water, and butter in the pan. Cook over medium heat until the mixture boils. Clip a candy thermometer to the inside of the pan; do not let the tip of the thermometer touch the bottom of the pan. Lower the heat and cook the sugar mixture to 275°F (25 to 30 minutes); the mixture will be very bubbly. Stir regularly throughout the cooking.

Stir in the peanuts and continue cooking until the mixture reaches 295°F. Working quickly, remove the pan from the heat and add the baking soda, stirring to blend. Pour the hot candy onto the lined baking sheets; it should be ¼ to ½ inch thick. While the brittle is still warm, sprinkle with the sea salt.

Let the brittle cool until completely firm, about 2 hours. Crack the brittle into 2- to 3-inch pieces.

MAKES
18
PRALINES

ACTIVE TIME
30 MINS

○ TOTAL TIME
30 MINS

PRALINES

❋

ALTHOUGH THEY ARE NAMED for a seventeenth-century French diplomat, César, duc de Choiseul, comte du Plessis-Praslin, these dropped sugar candies are all-American. Sometimes called pecan candy in New Orleans, they were hawked on the streets by African American candy sellers who easily appealed to the city's sweet tooth. The American praline has culinary cousins throughout the hemisphere, and a similar candy is called monkey meat in Charleston, South Carolina, *tablettes de coco* in the French Caribbean, and *pé de moleque* in Brazil. The nut changes with the geography, but the sweet-dropped patty embedded with nuts is the same.

1¼ cups granulated sugar

1 cup packed light brown sugar

6 tablespoons salted butter

½ cup half-and-half

1½ tablespoons vanilla extract, preferably Bourbon vanilla

1½ cups shelled jumbo pecans

Line a baking sheet with parchment paper.

In a deep, heavy saucepan, combine the granulated sugar, brown sugar, butter, and half-and-half. Cook over medium heat until the mixture boils, stirring often with a wooden spoon. Clip a candy thermometer to the inside of the pan: do not let the thermometer's tip touch the bottom of the pan.

Once the boiling sugar reaches 240°F, lower the heat to maintain that temperature and cook for 3 minutes longer. Add the vanilla extract and stir well.

Remove the pan from the heat and stir in the pecans. Continue to stir until the mixture begins to thicken. Thickening will occur as the sugars begin to cool; a creamy texture will be achieved by the constant stirring.

Once thickened, spoon the warm mixture onto the prepared baking sheet, forming 2½-inch praline clusters. Let the pralines cool to room temperature. Store in an airtight container at room temperature.

HIBISCUS & GINGER
SWEET TEA

HIBISCUS, WHICH IS KNOWN as sorrel or roselle in the Caribbean, *flor de Jamaica* in Mexico, *bissap* in Senegal, and *karkade* in Egypt, is the fresh or dried pod of *Hibiscus sabdariffa*, a plant native to West Africa. The bright red pods have long been valued for making hot and cold drinks and in folk medicine.

CHEF'S NOTE
Dried hibiscus flowers can be found in specialty groceries, health food stores, and Caribbean and Hispanic markets under one of its many names.

12 cups water

4 ounces fresh ginger, peeled and sliced

2 cups dried hibiscus flowers (*flor de Jamaica*)

⅔ cup superfine sugar

½ cup fresh mint leaves, for garnish

In a large pot, bring the water to a boil. Add the ginger and hibiscus. Turn off the heat and let steep for 1 hour.

Strain through a fine-mesh strainer, pressing against the solids to extract as much liquid as possible. Stir the sugar into the tea and refrigerate for 3 to 4 hours, until well chilled.

Serve the tea over ice in large glasses and garnish with mint.

AGRICULTURAL
SOUTH

MAKES
3 qts.

ACTIVE TIME
15 MINS

🕐

TOTAL TIME
**5 HRS
15 MINS**

SPARKLING WATERMELON &
LEMON VERBENA

HERBAL TEAS HAVE LONG been a part of African American culinary life, with cooks knowing just which one to use for digestion, to aid sleep, or to cure a cough. This recipe mixes watermelon juice with a simple syrup flavored with refreshing, calming lemon verbena for a cool drink that sparkles with the addition of seltzer or becomes alcoholic when mixed with Prosecco.

SYRUP

1 cup superfine sugar

¾ cup cold water

½ cup packed fresh lemon verbena leaves, plus more for garnish

COOLER

6 cups seedless watermelon, diced, plus small slices for garnish

1 (750-ml) bottle Prosecco or seltzer water

Juice of 1 lime

TO MAKE THE SYRUP
Combine the sugar and water in a saucepan and bring to a quick boil. Remove from the heat and add the lemon verbena leaves. Let cool completely, then strain through fine-mesh strainer and refrigerate.

TO MAKE THE COOLER
In a blender, puree the watermelon. Strain the watermelon puree, reserving the juice.

Mix the watermelon juice with the Prosecco, lime juice, and ½ cup of the syrup (add more if desired). Serve well chilled, garnishing each glass with a thin slice of watermelon and some lemon verbena leaves.

CONTINENTAL
UNITED STATES

MAKES
ABOUT
6 cups

ACTIVE TIME
20 MINS

🕐

TOTAL TIME
30 MINS

SWEET CHERRY
LEMONADE

CONTINENTAL
UNITED STATES

MAKES
2½ qts.

ACTIVE TIME
45 MINS
🕐
TOTAL TIME
**6 HRS
45 MINS**

LEMONADE IS POPULAR throughout the South, and the addition of homemade sweet cherry syrup turns it red, making it an ideal drink for Juneteenth picnics and celebrations. Red drinks are traditional at June-teenth events and may recall the celebratory hibiscus and kola nut teas of West Africa.

SWEET CHERRY SYRUP

1 pound pitted fresh
or frozen Bing cherries

¾ cup sugar

1 cup water

LEMONADE

1½ cups sugar

8 cups cold water, divided

1½ cups freshly squeezed
lemon juice, about 10 lemons

2 lemons, thinly sliced
and seeded, for garnish

TO MAKE THE SWEET CHERRY SYRUP

Combine the cherries, sugar, and water in a saucepan, bring to a simmer, and simmer for 15 minutes. Remove from the heat and strain through a fine-mesh strainer, pressing against the solids to extract as much syrup as possible. Pour into a bottle and chill well before using.

TO MAKE THE LEMONADE

Combine the sugar and 1 cup of the water in a saucepan. Bring to a boil over medium-high heat, reduce to a simmer, and simmer, stirring occasionally, until the sugar is completely dissolved, 2 to 3 minutes. Remove from the heat and allow to cool to room temperature.

Add the lemon juice and the remaining 7 cups water to the cooled sugar water and mix well. Refrigerate for 4 to 6 hours, until well chilled.

Serve the chilled lemonade over ice in tall glasses. Invite guests to sweeten it to their liking with the Sweet Cherry Syrup.

BASICS

**CHICKEN LIVERS & GRITS
WITH HAM & TOMATO GRAVY**

Opposite, top: Young men on a wagon filled with corn at the Bordentown School in Bordentown, New Jersey, ca. 1935. Photograph by Lewis Wickes Hine.

Opposite, bottom: Two women in a Harlem, New York, bakery, ca. 1960. Photograph by Lloyd W. Yearwood.

Above: Postcard of a woman carrying fruit in the Bahamas, early twentieth century.

BASICS

Creole Spice Blend / **196**

Barbecue Dry Rub / **196**

Wet Jerk Rub / **197**

Alabama White Barbecue Sauce / **197**

Brines / **198**

Poultry Brine / **198**

Stocks / **199**

Crab Stock / **199**

Chicken Stock / **200**

Ham & Pork Stock / **200**

Veal Stock / **201**

Vegetable Stock / **201**

Gribiche Sauce / **202**

Aioli / **202**

Stone-Ground Grits / **203**

CREOLE SPICE BLEND

MAKES

1 cup

ACTIVE TIME
10 MINS
🕙
TOTAL TIME
10 MINS

2 tablespoons sweet
Hungarian paprika

¼ cup celery salt

2 tablespoons fine sea salt

2 tablespoons ground black pepper

2 tablespoons garlic powder

2 tablespoons onion powder

1 tablespoon ground allspice

4 teaspoons cayenne pepper

Warm a nonstick skillet over low heat. Add the paprika and lightly toast to develop its full flavor. Actively stir the paprika for 3 minutes, making sure not to allow the spice to burn. Transfer the paprika to a small bowl and let cool.

Once the paprika has cooled to room temperature, whisk in all the remaining ingredients until well mixed.

Transfer to an airtight container. The blend will keep for up to 3 months.

BARBECUE DRY RUB

MAKES

2½ cups

ACTIVE TIME
10 MINS
🕙
TOTAL TIME
10 MINS

½ cup sweet Hungarian paprika

½ cup ground black pepper

½ cup turbinado sugar

¼ cup kosher salt

¼ cup dry English mustard

¼ cup onion powder

¼ cup garlic powder

2 teaspoons cayenne pepper

Warm a nonstick skillet over low heat. Add the paprika and lightly toast to develop its full flavor. Actively stir the paprika for 3 minutes, making sure not to allow the spice to burn. Transfer the paprika to a medium bowl and let cool.

When the paprika has cooled to room temperature, whisk in all the remaining ingredients until well mixed.

Transfer to an airtight container. The dry rub will keep for up to 3 months.

WET JERK RUB

MAKES
2 cups

ACTIVE TIME
25 MINS

🕐

TOTAL TIME
25 MINS

4 large garlic cloves

1 large yellow onion, chopped

3 scallions, white and light green parts, chopped

1 tablespoon fresh thyme leaves

5 tablespoons fresh cilantro, chopped

1 tablespoon fresh ginger, peeled and chopped

1 Scotch bonnet or habanero pepper, seeded

2 tablespoons freshly squeezed lime juice

1 teaspoon finely grated lime zest

¼ cup cold water

2 tablespoons packed dark brown sugar

1 tablespoon Dijon mustard

1 tablespoon whole allspice berries

2 cinnamon sticks, broken into pieces

⅛ teaspoon freshly grated nutmeg

2 tablespoons soy sauce

¼ cup peanut or vegetable oil

1 tablespoon sea salt

Combine all the ingredients in a food processor or blender and process until fully blended. Transfer to an airtight container and refrigerate for up to 2 weeks.

ALABAMA WHITE BARBECUE SAUCE

MAKES
6 cups

ACTIVE TIME
15 MINS

🕐

TOTAL TIME
20 MINS
PLUS
REFRIGERATE
OVERNIGHT

2 cups mayonnaise, preferably Duke's

6 tablespoons cider vinegar

2 tablespoons freshly squeezed lemon juice

¼ cup sugar

¼ cup freshly ground black pepper

¼ cup sour cream

1 teaspoon Worcestershire sauce

1 tablespoon kosher salt

1 teaspoon hot sauce

2 tablespoons grated prepared horseradish

Combine all the ingredients in a medium bowl and whisk until fully incorporated. Transfer to an airtight container and refrigerate overnight to allow the flavors to develop. The sauce will keep in the refrigerator for up to 3 days.

BRINES

Brines serve a few functions in the kitchen. They are flavor enhancers, allowing salt, spices, and herbs to permeate the meat or fish. They also assist in moisture retention throughout the cooking process. One popular example of this is the technique of brining a Thanksgiving turkey. Another function is as a preservative, as when used in preparing corned beef, deli meats, or pickled vegetables.

Brines typically include water; kosher or sea salt (never iodized); a sweetner such as sugar, honey, maple syrup, molasses, or a combination; and herbs and spices.

Brining time is determined by the size and weight of the item being brined. For example, chicken for deep-frying should be brined only overnight, while a Thanksgiving turkey is usually brined for several days.

Because brines are always used on raw ingredients, it is critical for food safety never to reuse a brine. They are intended for single use only.

POULTRY BRINE

MAKES

1 gal.

ACTIVE TIME
15 MINS

🕐

TOTAL TIME
**2 HRS
15 MINS**

4 quarts cold water, divided

1¼ cups salt

¾ cup sugar

1 tablespoon onion powder

1 tablespoon garlic powder

1½ teaspoons freshly ground black pepper

2 bay leaves

Pour 2 quarts of the water into a large stockpot and reserve the other half at room temperature. Add the salt, sugar, onion powder, garlic powder, pepper, and bay leaves to the pot and bring to a boil. Reduce the heat to a simmer and simmer for 5 minutes.

Remove the stockpot from the stovetop and pour in the remaining 2 quarts of water.

Cool the brine in the refrigerator for several hours until it reaches a temperature of 40°F. Once cool, the brine is ready to use.

STOCKS

Stocks are the foundation of soups, stews, and sauces in both professional and home kitchens. They help create the underlying flavor profiles of the food we cook.

When making a stock, the most important factor is the freshness of the ingredients used. The key components of a stock are bones, mirepoix (a mixture of carrot, onion, and celery), and aromatic herbs.

Whether preparing a meat, poultry, or seafood stock, be sure to obtain your bones and shells from a local butcher or fishmonger. Bones from younger animals have a higher gelatin content, which will yield a fuller-bodied stock.

Vegetable stocks, which require a shorter cooking time than poultry or meat stock, should always be made with nonstarchy vegetables. In addition to mushroom trimmings, dried mushrooms can significantly enhance the body of a vegetable stock.

STOCK-MAKING TIPS

o Always use the freshest ingredients.
o Obtain the bones from a local butcher or fish dealer.
o Rinse the bones with fresh water prior to preparing the stock.
o Start the stock with cold water.
o Always simmer, never boil, a stock
o Skim off and discard fats and impurities throughout the cooking process.
o Cooking times: vegetable stock, 1 hour; fish and shellfish stock, 1 to 1½ hours; chicken stock, 3 to 4 hours; veal stock, 8 to 12 hours.
o Once done, strain well and rapidly cool the stock using an ice bath.
o Store in the refrigerator for up to 4 day, or freeze for up to 1 month.

The effort put into making a high-quality homemade stock is well worth it, as many store-bought stocks are high in sodium and lack good flavor.

CRAB STOCK

MAKES

4 cups

ACTIVE TIME
25 MINS

🕐

TOTAL TIME
**1 HR
25 MINS**

1 tablespoon olive oil

1 tablespoon butter

2 pounds crab shells (may be available from fish dealers), coarsely chopped or cracked

1 yellow onion, finely diced

4 garlic cloves, coarsely chopped

3 celery stalks, finely diced

2 tablespoons tomato paste

2 teaspoons Old Bay seasoning

1 cup white wine

2 cups crushed tomatoes

3 bay leaves

1 tablespoon black peppercorns

5 fresh thyme sprigs

10 cups cold water

In a large soup pot, heat the oil and butter. Once they begin to sizzle, add the crab shells. With a wooden spoon, stir the shells to ensure they do not burn, and cook for 3 to 4 minutes.

Add the onion, garlic, and celery to the shells and cook until the vegetables begin to turn translucent, about 5 minutes. Then add the tomato paste and stir until the shells are coated and the tomato paste develops a rich aroma. Add the Old Bay seasoning and cook for another minute, stirring regularly. Now add the white wine and simmer for 5 minutes, until it has reduced by half.

Add the crushed tomatoes, bay leaves, peppercorns, thyme, and water. Gently simmer for 1 hour, skimming off any foam and fat throughout the process.

Strain the stock through a fine-mesh strainer and cool immediately.

Use the stock within 3 days or freeze for up to 1 month.

CHICKEN STOCK

MAKES

4 qts.

ACTIVE TIME
30 MINS
🕐
TOTAL TIME
**4 HRS
30 MINS**

10 pounds chicken bones (backs, wings, necks, and feet, if available)

4 quarts cold water

2 carrots, diced

2 celery stalks, sliced

1 large yellow onion, chopped

1 large leek, white and light green parts, washed well and sliced

1 head garlic, cut in half horizontally

1 bunch fresh parsley

3 bay leaves

½ bunch fresh thyme

1 tablespoon sea salt

1 teaspoon black peppercorns

Thoroughly rinse the chicken bones. Transfer them to a large stockpot and cover with the water. Bring to a simmer and cook for 45 minutes. Maintain a slow, gentle simmer, skimming off impurities and fat from the surface. Do not allow the stock to boil.

Next add the vegetables, herbs, and salt and peppercorns and gently simmer for 3¼ more hours. Continue skimming off the fat throughout the cooking.

Strain the stock through a fine-mesh strainer and cool immediately. Use the stock within 4 days or freeze for up to 1 month.

HAM & PORK STOCK

MAKES

4 qts.

ACTIVE TIME
**1 HR
30 MINS**
🕐
TOTAL TIME
**10 HRS
30 MINS**

5 pounds fresh pork bones (neck, spine, or leg; do not use country ham bones)

3 tablespoons vegetable oil

2 yellow onions, chopped

2 carrots, sliced

2 celery stalks

5 garlic cloves

8 quarts cold water, plus 1 cup to deglaze pot

2 smoked ham hocks

3 fresh thyme sprigs

3 bay leaves

2 tablespoons black peppercorns

1 teaspoon juniper berries

Preheat the oven to 350°F.

Thoroughly rinse the pork bones. Put the bones in a large roasting pan and toss with the vegetable oil to coat well. Roast for 45 minutes. Add the onions, carrots, celery, and garlic and roast for another 20 minutes, until the bones and vegetables are golden brown.

Transfer the bones to a large stockpot. Drain off any fat in the roasting pan, leaving the vegetables in the pan. Add the 1 cup water to the roasting pan and heat on the stovetop for 5 minutes. Remove the pan from the heat. With a wooden spoon, scrape all the browned bits from the pan bottom, then add the contents of the roasting pan to the stockpot. Pour in the 8 quarts water and bring to a simmer. Cook for 1 hour, maintaining a gentle, steady simmer and skimming off impurities and fat from the surface. Do not allow the stock to boil.

After the hour of simmering, add the ham hocks, thyme, bay leaves, peppercorns, and juniper berries cook over low heat for 8 hours longer.

Strain the stock through a fine-mesh sieve and cool immediately. Use the stock within 4 days or freeze for up to 1 month.

VEAL STOCK

MAKES

6 qts.

ACTIVE TIME
45 MINS

TOTAL TIME
1 DAY

10 pounds veal bones (knuckles and shins), split

½ cup vegetable oil

1 (6-ounce) can tomato paste

3 yellow onions, coarsely chopped

2 carrots, coarsely chopped

1 head garlic, cut in half horizontally

3 celery stalks, sliced

12 quarts cold water

2 cups white wine

1 bunch fresh parsley

½ bunch fresh thyme

2 tablespoons sea salt

1 tablespoon black peppercorns

Preheat the oven to 350°F.

Thoroughly rinse the veal bones. Put the bones in a large roasting pan and toss with the vegetable oil to coat well. Roast for 20 minutes, until a light golden brown. Add the tomato paste, onions, carrots, garlic, and celery and stir well to coat the tomato paste and vegetables in the pan drippings. Return to the oven for another 25 minutes, until the bones develop a rich caramelized color. Remove the roasting pan but leave the oven on.

Transfer the bones and vegetables to a large stockpot. Add the water, place on the stovetop, and bring to a simmer. While the bones are simmering, add the white wine to the roasting pan and stir to loosen any browned bits from the pan bottom. Return the pan to the oven for 10 minutes and cook until the wine has reduced by half. Then add the wine, pan drippings, parsley, thyme, salt, and peppercorns to the stockpot and simmer over low heat for at least 8 hours and up to 12 hours. Periodically skim off excess fat. Do not allow the stock to boil.

Strain the stock through a fine-mesh strainer and cool immediately. Use the stock within 4 days or freeze for up to 1 month.

VEGETABLE STOCK

MAKES

4 qts.

ACTIVE TIME
20 MINS

TOTAL TIME
1 HR 40 MINS

1 pound yellow onions

6 shallots

2 tablespoons olive oil

1 pound plum tomatoes, quartered

8 ounces carrots

1 parsnip

8 ounces celery stalks

8 ounces button mushrooms

3 leeks, white and light green parts

2 ounces dried mushrooms, such as shiitake, cèpes, or a combination

1 head garlic, cut in half horizontally

3 bay leaves

4 fresh thyme sprigs

6 fresh parsley stems

8 black peppercorns

1 teaspoon sea salt

5 quarts cold water

Preheat the oven to 400°F.

Leaving the skins on—they will add flavor and color to the stock—cut the onions and shallots into quarters. Toss with the olive oil and place in a large roasting pan. Roast for 15 minutes, until golden brown. Add the quartered tomatoes and roast for 15 minutes longer.

While the onions are roasting, peel the carrots and parsnip and cut into large dice along with the celery and button mushrooms.

Combine the leeks and the roasted vegetables in a large stockpot. Add the carrots, parsnip, celery, fresh and dried mushrooms, garlic, bay leaves, thyme, parsley stems, peppercorns, salt, and water. Bring to a steady simmer and cook for 1 hour, periodically skimming off any froth from the surface.

Strain the stock through a fine-mesh strainer and cool immediately. Use the stock within 4 days or freeze for up to 1 month.

GRIBICHE SAUCE

MAKES

1½ cups

ACTIVE TIME
10 MINS

🕐

TOTAL TIME
10 MINS

1 cup mayonnaise, preferably Duke's

½ cup fresh chervil, chopped

¼ cup fresh chives, chopped

1 shallot, finely minced

2 hard-boiled eggs, finely chopped

6 cornichons, chopped

2 teaspoons capers, chopped

2 teaspoons Dijon mustard

¼ teaspoon cayenne pepper

Salt

Freshly ground black pepper

Combine the mayonnaise, chervil, chives, shallot, eggs, cornichons, capers, mustard, and cayenne in a medium bowl and whisk together until well blended. Season to taste with salt and pepper.

AIOLI

MAKES

2¼ cups

ACTIVE TIME
15 MINS

🕐

TOTAL TIME
15 MINS

4 garlic cloves

3 large egg yolks

2 teaspoons water

½ teaspoon fine sea salt

1½ cups extra-virgin olive oil

1 tablespoon freshly squeezed lemon juice

Cayenne pepper

Peel the garlic cloves, split them in half, and remove any green sprouts. Place the garlic on a cutting board, smash them with the flat of a chef's knife, and chop to a paste: You should have about 1 tablespoon.

In a medium bowl, combine the garlic paste, egg yolks, water, and salt. Whisk until smooth and creamy. Gradually add the oil while whisking continuously. The oil must be added in a thin, slow, steady stream while whisking to create a thick emulsion. Whisk in the lemon juice, season to taste with cayenne, and then season with additional salt if needed.

VARIATION: **To make a red pepper aioli,** add 3 ounces of very finely chopped Spanish piquillo peppers or other fire-roasted red peppers and additional cayenne to taste.

STONE-GROUND GRITS

SERVES

4 to 6

ACTIVE TIME
15 MINS

🕐

TOTAL TIME
1 DAY
PLUS
OVERNIGHT
SOAKING OF
THE GRITS

2½ cups artisanal stone-ground grits (coarse ground, yellow or white)

8 cups cold water

½ cup half-and-half

2 tablespoons butter

1 teaspoon kosher salt

THE NIGHT BEFORE

Pour the grits into a large bowl and cover with the water. Briefly stir, then allow to rest for about 10 minutes. During this time some corn hulls might rise to the top; if so, skim them off using a slotted spoon. Transfer the grits to the refrigerator to soak overnight.

THE NEXT DAY

Transfer the grits and water to a pot large enough to accommodate the expansion of the grits during cooking. Cook over high heat, stirring continuously until the grits reach a boil. Then reduce the heat to the lowest setting and gently cook, covered, for 1 hour. Stir every 9 or 10 minutes to prevent scorching.

After an hour of cooking, the grits should be done. But as cooking times vary, taste the grits to determine whether they are cooked. They should be creamy and tender.

In a separate saucepan, bring the half-and-half to a quick boil and immediately remove it from the heat. Finish the grits with the half-and-half and butter and season with the salt. Serve immediately.

RECITES BY REGION

AGRICULTURAL SOUTH

Bacon-Wrapped Pan-Roasted Pork Chops / 114

Banana Pudding / 185

Benne Seed Flatbread Crisps / 157

Bourbon Pecan Pie / 169

Brunswick Stew / 68

Buttermilk Biscuits / 152

Buttermilk Fried Chicken / 103

Buttermilk Tea Cakes / 176

Charleston Pecan Chewies / 181

Chesapeake Corn & Crab Chowder / 60

Chicken Livers & Grits
with Ham & Tomato Gravy / 99

Chocolate Chess Pie / 165

Chow-Chow / 135

Classic Peanut Brittle / 186

Corn Pudding / 39

Cowpea & Collard Soup / 65

"Cracklin'" Corn Bread / 147

Deviled Eggs / 137

Fried Green Tomatoes / 38

Fried Okra / 41

Ginger & Brown Sugar Candied Sweet Potatoes / 42

Hibiscus & Ginger Sweet Tea / 189

Hickory-Smoked Barbecued Chicken / 109

Hickory-Smoked Pork Shoulder / 112

Hoppin' John / 46

Hot Water Corn Bread / 150

Lemon Curd Blueberry Tart / 171

Limpin' Susan / 120

Maryland Crab Cakes / 81

Mixed Greens with Baby Turnips / 37

Okra & Tomato Soup / 64

Pimento Cheese / 139

Potato Salad / 26

Red Velvet Cake / 182

Stewed Black-Eyed Peas / 35

Stewed Tomatoes & Okra / 30

Sweet Onion & Corn Hush Puppies
with Red Pepper Remoulade / 146

Sweet Potato Biscuits / 155

Sweet Potato Pie / 167

Tomato-Watermelon Salad / 20

Yellow Corn Bread / 151

Pickled Watermelon Rind / 131

CAFÉ SPECIALS

Black-Eyed Pea Hummus / 142

Collards, Tomato, & Cashew Stew / 61

Kale Sprouts with Sorghum & Benne Seeds / 33

Sticky Pork Ribs / 116

Vietnamese Spiced Chicken Wings / 96

CONTINENTAL UNITED STATES

Baby Kale Salad / 25

Baked Macaroni & Cheese / 45

Basic Pie Crust / 164

Coleslaw / 27

Dilly Green Beans / 133

Drop Biscuits / 153

Field Green Salad / 23

Fried Apple Hand Pies / 172

Johnnycakes / 149

Lemon-Glazed Pound Cake / 180

Lemon Meringue Pie / 170

Molasses Rum Raisin Cake / 177

Sea Salt-Spiced Cocktail Nuts / 140

Slow-Cooked Collards & Potlikker / 34

Sparkling Watermelon & Lemon Verbena / 189

Sweet Cherry Lemonade / 191

Sweet Pea Tendril Salad / 22

CREOLE COAST

Carolina Gold Rice Pilaf / 48

Catfish Po'boy / 85

Creole Spiced Boiled Peanuts / 141

Duck & Crawfish Gumbo / 62

Fried Croaker with Sweet Onion
& Corn Hush Puppies / 93

Frogmore Stew / 59

Louis Armstrong's Red Beans & Rice / 51

Pickled Gulf Shrimp / 29

Pralines / 188

Shrimp & Grits / 82

Spicy Pickled Okra / 134

Whole Grilled Snapper with Creole Sauce / 86

CULINARY COUSINS

Curried Goat / **119**

Jamaican Jerk Chicken / **101**

Rice & Pigeon Peas / **49**

Roti / **156**

Senegalese Peanut Soup / **71**

"Smoking Hot" Oxtail Pepper Pot / **69**

Trini Doubles / **121**

WESTERN RANGE

Barbecued Beef Brisket Sandwich / **110**

Black-Eyed Pea, Golden Corn,
& Chanterelle Empanadas / **122**

Charred Peach & Jalapeño Chutney / **136**

High Mesa Peach & Blackberry Cobbler / **175**

Pan-Roasted Rainbow Trout / **88**

Son-of-a-Gun Stew / **67**

Texas Caviar / **144**

NORTHERN STATES

Codfish Cakes / **87**

Hot Fried Chicken & Waffles / **105**

Joe Froggers / **178**

Salmon Croquettes / **90**

Smothered Turkey Grillades
with Fried Apples / **94**

Thomas Downing's NYC Oyster Pan Roast / **79**

Yankee Baked Beans / **43**

MENUS

JUNETEENTH
Texas Caviar

Barbecued Beef Brisket Sandwich

Potato Salad

Stewed Tomatoes & Okra

High Mesa Peach & Blackberry Cobbler

Sweet Cherry Lemonade

SUMMER BUFFET
Deviled Eggs

Frogmore Stew

Tomato-Watermelon Salad

Lemon Meringue Pie

Sparkling Watermelon
& Lemon Verbena

CALABASH CAROLINA FISH FRY
Dilly Green Beans

Spicy Pickled Okra

Fried Croaker

Coleslaw

Baby Kale Salad

Sweet Onion & Corn Hush Puppies
with Red Pepper Remoulade

Sweet Potato Pie

CARIBBEAN STREET FOOD
Trini Doubles

Curried Goat

Rice & Pigeon Peas

Roti

Molasses Rum Raisin Cake

NEW ORLEANS DINNER
Duck & Crawfish Gumbo

Whole Grilled Snapper with Creole Sauce

Louis Armstrong's Red Beans & Rice

Fried Green Tomatoes

Banana Pudding

THE SUNDAY TABLE
Chow-Chow

Buttermilk Fried Chicken

Baked Macaroni & Cheese

Slow-cooked Collards & Potlikker

Ginger & Brown Sugar Candied Sweet Potatoes

Yellow Corn Bread

Bourbon Pecan Pie

Hibiscus & Ginger Sweet Tea

FAMILY REUNION
Sea Salt-Spiced Roasted Cocktail Nuts

Pimento Cheese

Hickory-smoked Pork Shoulder

Hickory-smoked Barbecued Chicken

Limpin' Susan

Corn Pudding

Mixed Greens with Baby Turnips

Drop Biscuits

Lemon-glazed Pound Cake

Chocolate Chess Pie

MOTHER'S DAY BRUNCH
Pan-roasted Rainbow Trout

Carolina Gold Rice Pilaf

Stewed Black-eyed Peas

Pea Tendril Salad

Sweet Potato Biscuits

Buttermilk Tea Cakes

Pralines

VEGETARIAN FEAST
Dilly Green Beans

Black-eyed Pea, Golden Corn,
& Chanterelle Empanadas

Collard, Tomato, & Cashew Stew

Baby Kale Salad

Rice & Pigeon Peas

Fried Apple Hand Pies

ACKNOWLEDGMENTS

From Kinshasha Holman Conwill, Deputy Director, National Museum of African American History and Culture: The Sweet Home Café at the Smithsonian's National Museum of African American History and Culture is a collaborative effort. We at the museum—from the director to our curators, educators, and administrative staff—joined together to create a destination for visitors from around the corner and around the world that is in part a cultural culinary adventure and in part a communal experience. The result is a space suffused with the history and culture that this museum celebrates. This cookbook was another such collaboration. Our partners in the process of creating this wonderful book ensured that it too would be a celebration and a living tribute to our shared goal to animate black culture.

We are grateful to all who contributed to this volume. Our director, Lonnie G. Bunch III, was in many ways the "founder of the feast" that led to the development of the Sweet Home Café; thus his warmly personal introduction is a fitting beginning to this cookbook. Chief Curator Jacquelyn D. Serwer, a beloved cook in her own right, provided the lovely introduction that sets the tone for the pages that follow. Cultural anthropologist Jessica B. Harris laid the groundwork for the book's regional culinary themes; the author of the side and head notes that grace each chapter, she also helped to shape the book as a whole. Supervising Chef Albert G. Lukas created the book's delicious principal recipes and helped ensure that we never hit a false note in the recipes' authenticity and reliability. Executive Chef Jerome Grant contributed the marvelous "Culinary Cousins" recipes, which are a fundamental element of the Café and the book. Our thanks go out to all of the volunteers who tested these recipes in their home kitchens as well.

We are delighted to again partner with our colleagues at Smithsonian Books, including director Carolyn Gleason and senior editor Christina Wiginton, who deftly coordinated the editorial and development teams. Gary Tooth's gorgeous design ensured that the book is both beautiful and useful. The food photography team of photographer Scott Suchman, food stylist Lisa Cherkasky, and prop stylist Kristi Hunter ensured that the recipes look as delicious as they taste. Douglas Remley researched objects in our collections to make just the right pairings in the book. Cookbook team members Jacquelyn D. Serwer and John W. Franklin were joined in their efforts by scholars Elaine Nichols and Joanne Hyppolite to assure that the book remained true to both curatorial intent and gastronomic faithfulness. We cannot thank them enough.

The Café and this book are part of a larger relationship with our colleagues at Smithsonian Enterprises and Restaurant Associates. Restaurant Associates creatively completes the vision for the Sweet Home Café, and our collaboration has made the Café one of the Smithsonian's most successful restaurants to date. The support and enthusiasm of Carla Hall and Thompson Hospitality were also a part of the special ingredients that have made the Café such a triumph.

It is our profound wish that you, the reader of these pages, will be inspired to create meals that will nourish both you and your family and friends.

From Albert Lukas, Supervising Chef, Sweet Home Café: The Sweet Home Café has been a wonderfully exciting project, one in which we are able to celebrate the contributions of African American cooks to the development of iconic American foods.

I would like to thank my wife, Sarah, for all the encouragement and love she offers me. Additional thanks go to Ed Brown, Dick Cattani, George Conomos, and Marc Scheuer, along with the entire Restaurant Associates family; and to Lonnie G. Bunch III, the National Museum of African American History and Culture team, and our Smithsonian Enterprises partners all for their support, guidance, and encouragement throughout the developmental process and opening of the restaurant.

Final thanks to Chef Daniel Boulud, my mentor, along with my late grandfather Adam Metzger, who both taught me long ago about the important relationship between the food we prepare, eat, and serve and our collective history, culture, tradition, and family.

From Jessica B. Harris: I offer abundant thanks first to all the people, past and present, who created the tastes and tales celebrated here. I also thank my collaborators, Smithsonian Books, and especially the National Museum of African American History and Culture and its entire staff for allowing me to be a part of the adventure. Finally, I thank Jerome Grant and everyone at Restaurant Associates, who daily bring the vision so deliciously to life.

SELECTED BIBLIOGRAPHY

Bower, Anne. *African American Foodways: Explorations of History and Culture.* Urbana: University of Illinois Press, 2007.

Carney, Judith Ann. *Black Rice: The African Origins of Rice Cultivation in the Americas.* Cambridge, MA: Harvard University Press, 2001.

Carney, Judith Ann, and Richard Nicholas Rosomoff. *In the Shadow of Slavery: Africa's Botanical Legacy in the Atlantic World.* Berkeley: University of California Press, 2009.

Covey, Herbert C., and Dwight Eisnach. *What the Slaves Ate: Recollections of African American Foods and Foodways from the Slave Narratives.* Santa Barbara, CA: Greenwood Press/ABC-CLIO, 2009.

Craughwell, Thomas J. *Thomas Jefferson's Crème Brûlée: How a Founding Father and His Slave James Hemings Introduced French Cuisine to America.* Philadelphia: Quirk Books, 2012.

Deetz, Kelley Fanto. *Bound to the Fire: How Virginia's Enslaved Cooks Helped Invent American Cuisine.* Lexington: University Press of Kentucky, 2017.

Edge, John T. *The Potlikker Papers: A Food History of the Modern South.* New York: Penguin Press, 2017.

Gurley, Sue Harding. "From Steaming Hearths: The Transition from English Colonial Fare to African Foodways in the Coastal Regions of the American Upper South." Master's thesis, East Carolina University, 2014. http://hdl.handle.net/10342/4414.

Harris, Jessica B. *High on the Hog: A Culinary Journey from Africa to America.* New York: Bloomsbury, 2011.

Hess, Karen, and Louisa Cheves Smythe Stoney. *The Carolina Rice Kitchen: The African Connection.* Columbia: University of South Carolina Press, 1992.

Soul Food Junkies. Dir., written, and prod. Byron Hurt. Alexandria, VA: PBS, 2013. 63 min.

Littlefield, Daniel C. *Rice and Slaves: Ethnicity and the Slave Trade in Colonial South Carolina.* Illini Books ed. Urbana: University of Illinois Press, 1991.

Miller, Adrian. *The President's Kitchen Cabinet: The Story of the African Americans Who Have Fed Our First Families, from the Washingtons to the Obamas.* Chapel Hill: University of North Carolina Press, 2017.

Miller, Richard E. *The Messman Chronicles: African Americans in the U.S. Navy, 1932–1943.* Annapolis, MD: Naval Institute Press, 2004.

Opie, Frederick Douglass. *Hog & Hominy: Soul Food from Africa to America.* New York: Columbia University Press, 2008.

———. *Southern Food and Civil Rights: Feeding the Revolution.* Charleston, SC: American Palate/History Press, 2017.

Tipton-Martin, Toni. *The Jemima Code: Two Centuries of African American Cookbooks.* Austin: University of Texas Press, 2015.

Twitty, Michael. *The Cooking Gene: A Journey through African American Culinary History in the Old South.* New York: Amistad/HarperCollins, 2017.

Wallach, Jennifer Jensen, Psyche A. Williams-Forson, and Rebecca Sharpless. *Dethroning the Deceitful Pork Chop: Rethinking African American Foodways from Slavery to Obama.* Fayetteville: University of Arkansas Press, 2015.

Warner, Mark S. *Eating in the Side Room: Food, Archaeology, and African American Identity.* Gainesville: University Press of Florida, 2015.

Williams-Forson, Psyche A. *Building Houses out of Chicken Legs: Black Women, Food, and Power.* Chapel Hill: University of North Carolina Press, 2006.

Witt, Doris. *Black Hunger: Soul Food and America.* Minneapolis: University of Minnesota Press, 2004.

INDEX

Page numbers in **bold** indicate photographs and other illustrations.

A

African American cookbooks, 18, 56, 135, 162. *See also specific authors and titles*

African American cooks, 11; cowboy cooks, 67; enslaved chefs, 11, 76; home cooks, 11, 12, 13, 18, 76; in the South, 18, 76, 188; in the West, 56, 135. *See also* African American entrepreneurs and eating establishments; *specific people by name*

African American entrepreneurs and eating establishments: in the North, 12, **75**, 79, 84, 131, **160**, 162, 178, 182; photographs of, **55**, **74**, **161**; in the South, 12, 18, **19**, **70**, 76, 103, 141; in the West, 56. *See also* African American cooks; *specific cities and restaurants*

African American foodways, 11–13; in the Agricultural South, 76–77; barbecue, 107; in the Creole Coast, 18–19; Culinary Cousins, 128–29; in the Northern States, 162–63; in the Western Range, 56–57. *See also specific foods*

African Americans, stereotypes of, 76, 132

African foods and influences, 18, 128; benne seeds, 33; field peas, 142; hibiscus flowers, 189; okra, 30, 32, 41, 134; peanuts, 70; rice, 18, 47, 128; watermelon, 132

Agricultural South, 76–77; list of recipes from, 204

agriculture: home gardens, 12, 18; rice cultivation, 18, 47, **47**, 128; sugarcane cultivation, 177. *See also other specific foods*

Aioli, 202: Pimento Cheese Aioli, 41; Red Pepper Aioli, 202; Roast Tomato Aioli, 38

Alabama White Barbecue Sauce, 197

Alleyne, Dionne, 26

almonds: Sea Salt–Spiced Cocktail Nuts, 140

Amy Ruth's, 182

Anderson, Henry Clay, **77**

apples: Fried Apple Hand Pies, 172–73, **173**; Smothered Turkey Grillades with Fried Apples, 94–95, **95**

Armstrong, Louis, 51; Louis Armstrong's Red Beans and Rice, **50**, 51

Asian culinary influences: East Indian culinary influence, 119, 121, 156; Sticky Pork Ribs, 116–17, **117**. *See also* curried dishes

B

Baby Kale Salad, **24**, 25

bacon: Bacon-Wrapped Pan-Roasted Pork Chops, 114, **115**; "Cracklin'" Corn Bread, 147; Limpin' Susan, 120; Mixed Greens with Baby Turnips, 37; Red Beans and Rice, Louis Armstrong's, **50**, 51

Baked Beans, Yankee, 43

Baked Macaroni and Cheese, **44**, 45

Banana Pudding, **184**, 185

barbecue, 107; Barbecued Beef Brisket Sandwich, 110–11, **111**; Barbecue Dry Rub, 196; Hickory-Smoked Barbecue Chicken, **108**, 109; Hickory-Smoked Pork Shoulder, 112–13; Jamaican Jerk Chicken, 101; Sticky Pork Ribs, 116–17, **117**

barbecue sauce: Alabama White Barbecue Sauce, 197; Eastern North Carolina–Style Barbecue Sauce, 112

barley: Son-of-a-Gun Stew, **66**, 67

Baruch, Ruth-Marion, **107**

basic recipes, 192–203; Aioli, 202; Alabama White Barbecue Sauce, 197; Barbecue Dry Rub, 196; Basic Pie Crust, 164; Chicken Stock, 200; Crab Stock, 199; Creole Spice Blend, 196; Gribiche Sauce, 202; Ham and Pork Stock, 200; Poultry Brine, 198; Stone-Ground Grits, 203; Veal Stock, 201; Vegetable Stock, 201; Wet Jerk Rub, 197

beans: Dilly Green Beans, **130**, 133; limas, in Brunswick Stew, 68; Red Beans and Rice, Louis Armstrong's, **50**, 51; Yankee

Baked Beans, 43

Beaufort Stew (Frogmore Stew), 58, 59

beef: Barbecued Beef Brisket Sandwich, 110–11, **111**; "Smoking Hot" Oxtail Pepper Pot, 69; Son-of-a-Gun Stew, **66**, 67

bell peppers: Chow-Chow, **130**, 135; Pimento Cheese, **138**, 139; Red Pepper Aioli, 202; Red Pepper Remoulade, Sweet Onion and Corn Hush Puppies with, 146

benne seeds, 33; Benne Seed Flatbread Crisps, 157; Kale Sprouts with Sorghum and Benne, 33; Sea Salt–Spiced Cocktail Nuts, 140

Bentzon, Peter, **127**

Bernoon, Emmanuel "Manna," 162

biscuits: Buttermilk Biscuits, 152; Drop Biscuits, 153; Sweet Potato Biscuits, **154**, 155

blackberries: High Mesa Peach and Blackberry Cobbler, **174**, 175

black-eyed peas, 143; Baby Kale Salad with, **24**, 25; Black-Eyed Pea, Golden Corn, and Chanterelle Empanadas, 122–23, **123**; Black-Eyed Pea Hummus, 142; Hoppin' John, 46; Stewed Black-Eyed Peas, 35; Texas Caviar, 144, **145**

Blanche, Gustave III, **74**

blueberries: Lemon Curd Blueberry Tart, 171

Boiled Peanuts, Creole Spiced, 141

Boston Baked Beans, 43

bourbon: Bourbon Pecan Pie, **168**, 169; Spiced Sorghum Syrup with, 105–06

breads: Benne Seed Flatbread Crisps, 157; Buttermilk Biscuits, 152; "Cracklin'" Corn Bread, 147; Drop Biscuits, 153; Hot Water Corn Bread, 150; Johnnycakes, **148**, 149; Roti, 156; Sweet Onion and Corn Hush Puppies with Red Pepper Remoulade, 146; Sweet Potato Biscuits, **154**, 155; Yellow Corn Bread, 151

brines, 198; Poultry Brine, 198

Brittle, Peanut, 186, **187**

Brown, Joe, 178

Brown, Lucretia, 178

brown butter: Hazelnut Brown Butter
Sauce, Pan-Roasted Rainbow Trout
with, 88–89, **89**

Brown Sauce, 100; Bacon-Wrapped Pan-
Roasted Pork Chops with molasses
gravy, 114, **115**; Chicken Livers and
Grits with Ham and Tomato Gravy,
98, 99–100

Brunswick Stew, 68

Butler, Cleora, 56

buttermilk: Buttermilk Dressing, Baby
Kale Salad with, **24**, 25; Buttermilk
Biscuits, 152; Buttermilk Fried Chicken,
77, **102**, 103; Buttermilk Tea Cakes, 176;
"Cracklin'" Corn Bread, 147; Hot Fried
Chicken and Waffles, 105–106; Sweet
Potato Biscuits, **154**, 155; Red Velvet
Cake, **181**, 182; Yellow Corn Bread, 151

Buttermilk Biscuits, 152

Buttermilk Dressing, **24**, 25

Buttermilk Fried Chicken, **102**, 103–04

Buttermilk Tea Cakes, 176

C

cabbage: Chow-Chow, **130**, 135;
Coleslaw, 27

Café specials recipe list, 204

cakes, cornmeal: Hot Water Corn Bread,
150; Johnnycakes, **148**, 149

cakes, fish and seafood: Codfish Cakes, 87;
Maryland Crab Cakes, **80**, 81

cakes, sweet: Buttermilk Tea Cakes,
176; Lemon-Glazed Pound Cake, 180;
Molasses Rum Raisin Cake, 177; Red
Velvet Cake, 182–83, **183**

Candied Sweet Potatoes, with Ginger and
Brown Sugar, 42

candies: Peanut Brittle, 186, **187**;
Pralines, 188

Caribbean-influenced recipes: Curried
Goat, **118**, 119; Jamaican Jerk Chicken,
101; Rice and Pigeon Peas, 49; Roti, 156;
"Smoking Hot" Oxtail Pepper Pot, 69;
Trini Doubles, 121

Carolinas: Carolina fish fry menu, 207;
Carolina Gold Rice Pilaf, 48; Eastern
North Carolina–Style Barbecue
Sauce, 112; rice in, 18, 47, **47**. See also
Charleston (SC)

carrots: Coleslaw, 27; Sweet Pea Tendril
Salad, 22

Carver, George Washington, 70, 76, 142

cashews: Collard, Tomato, and Cashew
Stew, 61; Sea Salt–Spiced Cocktail Nuts,
140

cassareep, 69

casseroles: Baked Macaroni and Cheese,
44, 45; Corn Pudding, 39; Ginger
and Brown Sugar Candied Sweet
Potatoes, 42

caterers and catering companies,
18, 56, 162

Catfish Po'boy, 85

Caviar, Texas, 144, **145**

chanterelles: Black-Eyed Pea, Golden Corn,
and Chanterelle Empanadas, 122–23, **123**

Charleston (SC), 18, 82, 141, 188

Charleston Pecan Chewies, 181

Charred Peach and Jalapeño Chutney,
130, 136

cheese: Baked Macaroni and Cheese, **44**,
45; Pimento Cheese, **138**, 139; Pimento
Cheese Aioli, 41

chefs. See African American cooks;
specific individuals

Cherry Lemonade, **190**, 191

Chesapeake Corn and Crab Chowder, 60

Chess Pie, Chocolate, 165

chicken: brining, 198; Brunswick Stew, 68;
Buttermilk Fried Chicken, **102**, 103–04;
Chicken Livers and Grits with Ham and
Tomato Gravy, **98**, 99–100; Chicken
Stock, 200; fried, 76, 103, 105–06; Fried
Chicken and Waffles, Hot, 105–06;
Hickory-Smoked Barbecue Chicken,
108, 109; Jamaican Jerk Chicken, 101;
Vietnamese Spiced Chicken Wings,
96, **97**

chickpeas: Trini Doubles, 121

chile peppers: Charred Peach and Jalapeño
Chutney, **130**, 136; Chow-Chow, **130**,
135; Curried Goat, **118**, 119; "Smoking
Hot" Oxtail Pepper Pot, 69; Spicy
Pickled Okra, **130**, 134; Texas Caviar,
144, **145**; Trini Doubles, 121; Wet Jerk
Rub, 197

chocolate and cocoa: Chocolate Chess Pie,
165; Red Velvet Cake, 182–83, **183**

Chow-Chow, **130**, 135

Chowder, Corn and Crab, Chesapeake, 60

Chutney, Charred Peach and Jalapeño,
130, 136

civil rights movement restaurant sit-ins,
12, 13, 76

*Cleora's Kitchens: The Memoir of a Cook &
Eight Decades of Great American Food*
(Butler), 56

Cobbler, Peach and Blackberry, High Mesa,
174, 175

Cocktail Nuts, Sea Salt–Spiced, 140

Codfish Cakes, 87

Coleslaw, 27

collards, 34; Collard, Tomato, and Cashew
Stew, 61; Cowpea and Collard Soup, 65;
Slow-Cooked Collards and Potlikker, 34

cookies: Buttermilk Tea Cakes, 176;
Charleston Pecan Chewies, 181; Joe
Froggers, 178, **179**

corn: Baby Kale Salad with, **24**, 25; Black-
Eyed Pea, Golden Corn, and Chanterelle
Empanadas, 122–23, **123**; Brunswick
Stew, 68; Chesapeake Corn and Crab
Chowder, 60; Corn Pudding, 39;
Frogmore Stew, **58**, 59; Son-of-a-Gun
Stew, **66**, 67

corn breads: corn bread croutons, 25;
"Cracklin'" Corn Bread, 147; Hot Water
Corn Bread, 150; Johnnycakes, **148**, 149;
Sweet Onion and Corn Hush Puppies
with Red Pepper Remoulade, 146;
Yellow Corn Bread, 151

cornmeal and corn flour: Benne Seed
Flatbread Crisps, 157; Waffles, Fried
Chicken with, 105–06. See also corn
breads; grits

cowboy cooks, 67

cowpeas, 142; Cowpea and Collard Soup,
65. See also black-eyed peas; peas

crab: Chesapeake Corn and Crab Chowder,
60; Crab Stock, 199; Frogmore Stew, **58**,
59; Maryland Crab Cakes, **80**, 81

"Cracklin'" Corn Bread, 147

crawfish: Duck and Crawfish Gumbo,
62–63, **63**

Cream Cheese Frosting, Red Velvet Cake
with, 182–83, **183**

Creole Coast, 18–19; list of recipes from,
205

Creole Sauce, Whole Grilled Snapper
with, 86

Creole Spice Blend, 196

Creole Spiced Boiled Peanuts, 141

Croquettes, Salmon, 90–91

croutons, corn bread, 25

Crum, George, 162

cucumber, Field Green Salad with, 23

Culinary Cousins, 128–29; recipe list, 206

curried dishes: Collard, Tomato, and
Cashew Stew, 61; Curried Goat, **118**,
119; Senegalese Peanut Soup, 71; Trini
Doubles, 121

D

Denver (CO), 56

desserts. See sweets

Deviled Eggs, 137

Dilly Green Beans, **130**, 133

dips and spreads: Aioli, 202; Black-Eyed Pea Hummus, 142; Fresh Tomato Salsa, 122; Pimento Cheese, **138**, 139; Pimento Cheese Aioli, 41; Red Pepper Aioli, 202; Roast Tomato Aioli, 38. *See also* sauces

A Domestic Cook Book: Containing a Careful Selection of Useful Receipts for the Kitchen (Russell), 162

Doubles, Trini, 121

Downing's Oyster House, 12, 84

Dressing, Buttermilk, Baby Kale Salad with, **24**, 25

drinks: Hibiscus and Ginger Sweet Tea, 189; Sparkling Watermelon and Lemon Verbena, 189; Sweet Cherry Lemonade, **190**, 191

Drop Biscuits, 153

Dry Rub, Barbecue, 196

DuBois, W. E. B., 162

Duck and Crawfish Gumbo, 62–63, **63**

E

Eastern North Carolina–Style Barbecue Sauce, 112

East Indian foods and influences, 119, 121, 156. *See also* curried dishes

eggs, hard-boiled: Deviled Eggs, 137; Gribiche Sauce, 91, 202

empanadas, Black-Eyed Pea, Golden Corn, and Chanterelle Empanadas, 122–23, **123**

enslaved chefs, 11, 76

European culinary influences, 18

F

Field Green Salad, 23

field peas, 142. *See also* peas

fish: Catfish Po'boy, 85; Codfish Cakes, 87; Fried Croaker with Sweet Onion and Corn Hush Puppies, **92**, 93; Pan-Roasted Rainbow Trout, 88–89, **89**; Salmon Croquettes, 90–91; Whole Grilled Snapper with Creole Sauce, 86

Fisher, Abby, 56, 135

flatbreads: Benne Seed Flatbread Crisps, 157; Johnnycakes, **148**, 149; Roti, 156

Florida Avenue Grill, 12

Ford, Barney, 56

Freed, Leonard, **19**

fried foods: Black-Eyed Pea, Golden Corn, and Chanterelle Empanadas, 122–23, **123**; Buttermilk Fried Chicken, **102**,

103–04; chicken, 76, 103, 105–06; Fried Apple Hand Pies, 172–73, **173**; Fried Chicken and Waffles, Hot, 105–06; Fried Croaker with Sweet Onion and Corn Hush Puppies, **92**, 93; Fried Green Tomatoes, 38; Fried Okra, **40**, 41; Sweet Onion and Corn Hush Puppies with Red Pepper Remoulade, 146

Frogmore Stew, **58**, 59

G

ginger: Ginger and Brown Sugar Candied Sweet Potatoes, 42; Hibiscus and Ginger Sweet Tea, 189

Goat, Curried, **118**, 119

Gordonsville (VA), 76, 103

Grant, Jerome, 13

gravy: Ham and Tomato Gravy, Chicken Livers and Grits with, **98**, 99–100; molasses, Bacon-Wrapped Pan-Roasted Pork Chops with, 114, **115**

Green, Victor, *Green Book,* 12–13, **13**

Green Beans, Dilly, **130**, 133

greens: Collard, Tomato, and Cashew Stew, 61; Cowpea and Collard Soup, 65; Kale Sprouts with Sorghum and Benne, 33; Mixed Greens with Baby Turnips, **36**, 37; Slow-Cooked Collards and Potlikker, 34; *See also* salads

Greensboro lunch counter sit-in, 13, 76

green tomatoes: Chow-Chow, **130**, 135; Fried Green Tomatoes, 38

Gribiche Sauce, 91, 202; Codfish Cakes with, 87; Salmon Croquettes with, 90–91

grillades, 94; Smothered Turkey Grillades with Fried Apples, 94–95, **95**

grits: basic Stone-Ground Grits, 203; Chicken Livers and Grits with Ham and Tomato Gravy, **98**, 99–100; Shrimp and Grits, 82–83, **83**

grocery stores and markets, 12, 55, **160**, **163**

Gulf Shrimp, Pickled, **28**, 29

gumbos: about, 18, 30, 32, 128; Duck and Crawfish Gumbo, 62–63, **63**

gungo peas. *See* Pigeon Peas, Rice and

H

habanero peppers, 69. *See also* chile peppers

ham and ham hocks: Cowpea and Collard Soup, 65; Ham and Pork Stock, 200; Ham and Tomato Gravy, Chicken Livers

and Grits with, **98**, 99–100; Red Beans and Rice, Louis Armstrong's, **50**, 51; Slow-Cooked Collards and Potlikker, 34; Stewed Black-Eyed Peas, 35

Harlem (NYC), 55, 74, 105, 131, **160**, 182

Harris, Jessica B., 13

hazelnuts: Hazelnut Brown Butter Sauce, Pan-Roasted Rainbow Trout with, 88–89, **89**; Sea Salt–Spiced Cocktail Nuts, 140

Hemings, James, 76

Hercules, 11, 76

Hibiscus and Ginger Sweet Tea, 189

Hickory-Smoked Barbecue Chicken, **108**, 109

Hickory-Smoked Pork Shoulder, 112–13

High Mesa Peach and Blackberry Cobbler, **174**, 175

Hine, Lewis Wickes, **126**, **194**

hoecakes. *See* Johnnycakes

holidays: Juneteenth foods, 144, 207; New Year's Day foods, 35, 46, 142; Thanksgiving foods, 42, 167

Hot Water Corn Bread, 150

Hummus, Black-Eyed Pea, 142

Hunt's Cafe, **55**

Hurston, Zora Neale, 176

hush puppies: Fried Croaker with Sweet Onion and Corn Hush Puppies, **92**, 93; Sweet Onion and Corn Hush Puppies with Red Pepper Remoulade, 146

I

Indian culinary influences. *See* curried dishes; East Indian foods and influences; Native American foods and influences

J

Jackson, Mary A., **19**

jalapeño peppers: Charred Peach and Jalapeño Chutney, **130**, 136; *See also* chile peppers

Jamaican dishes: Curried Goat, **118**, 119; Jamaican Jerk Chicken, 101

Jefferson, Thomas, 32, 45, 76

jerk: Jamaican Jerk Chicken, 101; Wet Jerk Rub, 197

Joe Froggers, 178, **179**

Johnnycakes, **148**, 149

Johnson, Jason Miccolo, **163**

Johnson, John, **10**

Jones Bar-B-Q Diner, 12

Juneteenth foods, 144, 207

K

kale: Baby Kale Salad, **24**, 25; Kale Sprouts with Sorghum and Benne, 33; Mixed Greens with Baby Turnips, **36**, 37

L

LaBelle, Patti, **75**
Latin American culinary influences: Black-eyed Pea, Golden Corn, and Chanterelle Empanadas, 122–23, **123**
lemons: Lemon Curd Blueberry Tart, 171; Lemon-Glazed Pound Cake, 180; Lemon Meringue Pie, 170; Sweet Cherry Lemonade, **190**, 191
Lemon Verbena and Watermelon, Sparkline, 189
Lewis, Edna, 11, 76
lima beans: Brunswick Stew, 68
Limpin' Susan, 120
Livers, Chicken, and Grits, with Ham and Tomato Gravy, **98**, 99–100
Louis Armstrong's Red Beans and Rice, **50**, 51
Low Country boil (Frogmore Stew), **58**, 59
Lukas, Albert, 13
lunch counter sit-ins, **12**, 13, 76
Lyon, Danny, **12**

M

Macaroni and Cheese, Baked, **44**, 45
McNeill, Robert H., **160**
mafé, 71
main dishes, 72–123; Bacon-Wrapped Pan-Roasted Pork Chops, 114, **115**; Barbecued Beef Brisket Sandwich, 110–11, **111**; Black-eyed Pea, Golden Corn, and Chanterelle Empanadas, 122–23, **123**; Buttermilk Fried Chicken, **102**, 103–04; Catfish Po'boy, 85; Chicken Livers and Grits with Ham and Tomato Gravy, **98**, 99–100; Codfish Cakes, 87; Curried Goat, **118**, 119; Fried Chicken and Waffles, Hot, 105–06; Fried Croaker with Sweet Onion and Corn Hush Puppies, **92**, 93; Hickory-Smoked Barbecue Chicken, **108**, 109; Hickory-Smoked Pork Shoulder, 112–13; Jamaican Jerk Chicken, 101; Limpin' Susan, 120; Maryland Crab Cakes, **80**, 81; NYC Oyster Pan Roast, Thomas Downing's, 79; Pan-Roasted Rainbow Trout, 88–89, **89**; Salmon Croquettes, 90–91; Shrimp and Grits, 82–83, **83**;

Smothered Turkey Grillades with Fried Apples, 94–95, **95**; Sticky Pork Ribs, 116–17, **117**; Trini Doubles, 121; Vietnamese Spiced Chicken Wings, 96, **97**; Whole Grilled Snapper with Creole Sauce, 86, *See also* soups and stews
markets and grocery stores, 12, **55**, **160**, **163**
Marovich, Pete, **16–17**, **84**
Maryland Crab Cakes, **80**, 81
mayonnaise dips and sauces: Aioli, 202; Alabama White Barbecue Sauce, 197; Gribiche Sauce, 91, 202; Pimento Cheese, **138**, 139; Pimento Cheese Aioli, 41; Red Pepper Aioli, 202; Red Pepper Remoulade, Sweet Onion and Corn Hush Puppies with, 146; Roast Tomato Aioli, 38
meats. *See* barbecue; *specific meats*
menus, 207
Mixed Greens with Baby Turnips, **36**, 37
molasses: gravy, Bacon-Wrapped Pan-Roasted Pork Chops with, 114, **115**; Joe Froggers, 178, **179**; Molasses Rum Raisin Cake, 177
Monticello, 32. *See also* Jefferson, Thomas
Morris, Charles E., **57**
Moutoussamy-Ashe, Jeanne, **54**
mushrooms: Black-Eyed Pea, Golden Corn, and Chanterelle Empanadas, 122–23, **123**; Vegetable Stock with, 201
mustard greens: Mixed Greens with Baby Turnips, **36**, 37; Pan-Roasted Rainbow Trout stuffed with, 88–89, **89**

N

National Museum of African American History and Culture, 12–13
Native American foods and influences, 39, 149, 151
New Orleans, 18, 51, 84, 85, 94, 188; dinner menu from, 207
New Year's Day foods, 35, 142; Hoppin' John, 46
New York, 12, 79, 84, 162. *See also* Harlem
Northern States, 162–63; list of recipes from, 206
Northup, Anne Hampton, 162
nuts: Hazelnut Brown Butter Sauce, Pan-Roasted Rainbow Trout with, 88–89, **89**; Sea Salt–Spiced Cocktail Nuts, 140. *See also* peanuts; pecans
NYC Oyster Pan Roast, Thomas Downing's, 79

O

okra, 30, 32, 41, 134; Duck and Crawfish Gumbo, 62–63, **63**; Fried Okra, **40**, 41; Limpin' Susan, 120; Okra and Tomato Soup, 64; Spicy Pickled Okra, **130**, 134; Stewed Tomatoes and Okra, 30, **31**
Old Doll, 11
onions: Chow-Chow, **130**, 135; Coleslaw, 27; Sweet Onion and Corn Hush Puppies, 146;
Oxtail Pepper Pot, "Smoking Hot," 69
oysters, 85, 162; NYC Oyster Pan Roast, Thomas Downing's, 79

P

Patillo's Bar-B-Q, 12
peaches: Charred Peach and Jalapeño Chutney, **130**, 136; High Mesa Peach and Blackberry Cobbler, **174**, 175
peanuts, 70; Creole Spiced Boiled Peanuts, 141; Peanut Brittle, 186, **187**; Senegalese Peanut Soup, 71
peas, 143; Baby Kale Salad with black-eyed peas, **24**, 25; Black-Eyed Pea, Golden Corn, and Chanterelle Empanadas, 122–23, **123**; Black-Eyed Pea Hummus, 142; Cowpea and Collard Soup, 65; Hoppin' John, 46; Rice and Pigeon Peas, 49; Stewed Black-Eyed Peas, 35; Trini Doubles, 121. *See also* pea tendrils
pea tendrils: Sweet Pea Tendril Salad, 22
pecans, 140, 169; Bourbon Pecan Pie, **168**, 169; Charleston Pecan Chewies, 181; Pralines, 188; Sea Salt–Spiced Cocktail Nuts, 140; spiced, Field Green Salad with, 23
Pepper Pot, Oxtail, "Smoking Hot," 69
peppers. *See* bell peppers; chile peppers
Philadelphia, 162
pickles and preserves: Charred Peach and Jalapeño Chutney, **130**, 136; Chow-Chow, **130**, 135; Dilly Green Beans, **130**, 133; Pickled Gulf Shrimp, **28**, 29; Pickled Watermelon Rind, **130**, 131; Spicy Pickled Okra, **130**, 134
picnics, **10**, **77**, **126**
pie: Basic Pie Crust, 164; Bourbon Pecan Pie, **168**, 169; Chocolate Chess Pie, 165; Fried Apple Hand Pies, 172–73, **173**; Lemon Meringue Pie, 170; Sweet Potato Pie, **166**, 167
Pigeon Peas, Rice and, 49
pilafs, 18, 128; Carolina Gold Rice Pilaf, 48; Limpin' Susan, 120

Pimento Cheese, **138**, 139; Deviled Eggs with, 137; Pimento Cheese Aioli, 41

Pleasant, Mary Ellen, 56

pork: Bacon-Wrapped Pan-Roasted Pork Chops, 114, **115**; Ham and Pork Stock, 200; Hickory-Smoked Pork Shoulder, 112–13; Red Beans and Rice, Louis Armstrong's, **50**, 51; Sticky Pork Ribs, 116–17, **117**. *See also* bacon; ham; sausage

potatoes: Brunswick Stew, 68; Chesapeake Corn and Crab Chowder, 60; Frogmore Stew, **58**, 59; Potato Salad, 26; Son-of-a-Gun Stew, **66**, 67; Trini Doubles, 121

Potlikker, Slow-Cooked Collards and, 34

poultry: Poultry Brine, 198. *See also* chicken; duck; turkey

Pound Cake, Lemon-Glazed, 180

Pralines, 188

preserves. *See* pickles and preserves

Providence (RI), 162

pudding: Banana Pudding, **184**, 185; Corn Pudding, 39

purloos, 18. *See also* pilafs

R

rabbit: Brunswick Stew, 68

radishes: Sweet Pea Tendril Salad, 22

railroad cooks, **56–57**

Rainbow Trout, Pan-Roasted, 88–89, **89**

raisins: Molasses Rum Raisin Cake, 177

Randolph, Mary, 32, 45

Randolph, Patsy, 131

Raven, Cake Man, 182

Red Beans and Rice, Louis Armstrong's, **50**, 51

Red Pepper Aioli, 202

Red Pepper Remoulade: Catfish Po'boy with, 83; Sweet Onion and Corn Hush Puppies with, 146

Red Velvet Cake, 182–83, **183**

regional foodways and recipes: from Agricultural South, 76–77, 204; from Creole Coast, 18–19, 205; from Northern States, 162–63, 206; from Western Range, 56–57, 206

regional menus, 207

Remoulade, Red Pepper: Catfish Po'boy with, 83; Sweet Onion and Corn Hush Puppies with, 146

restaurants. *See* African American entrepreneurs and eating establishments; *specific restaurants and cities*

restaurant sit-ins, **12**, 13, 76

ribs: beef, Son-of-a-Gun Stew with, **66**, 67;

Sticky Pork Ribs, 116–17, **117**

rice, 18, 47, 128; Carolina Gold Rice Pilaf, 48; Hoppin' John, 46; Limpin' Susan, 120; Red Beans and Rice, Louis Armstrong's, **50**, 51; Rice and Pigeon Peas, 49

Richard, Lena, 18

Roast Tomato Aioli, 38

Roti, 156; Trini Doubles with, 121

rubs: Barbecue Dry Rub, 196; Wet Jerk Rub, 197

Rum Raisin Cake, Molasses, 177

Russell, Malinda, 162

S

salads: Baby Kale Salad, **24**, 25; Coleslaw, 27; Field Green Salad, 23; Potato Salad, 26; Sweet Pea Tendril Salad, 22; Texas Caviar, 144, **145**; Tomato-Watermelon Salad, 20, **21**

Salmon Croquettes, 90–91

Salsa, Fresh Tomato, 122

sandwiches: Barbecued Beef Brisket Sandwich, 110–11, **111**; Catfish Po'boy, 85

San Francisco (CA), 56

Saratoga Springs, New York, 162

sauces: Barbecue, Alabama White, 197; Barbecue, Eastern North Carolina–Style, 112; Brown Sauce, 100; Creole Sauce, Whole Grilled Snapper with, 86; Gribiche Sauce, 202; Hazelnut Brown Butter Sauce, Pan-Roasted Rainbow Trout with, 88–89, **89**; Red Pepper Remoulade, Catfish Po'boy with, 85; Red Pepper Remoulade, Sweet Onion and Corn Hush Puppies with, 146. *See also* dips and spreads; gravy

sausage: Frogmore Stew, **58**, 59

Schwartz, Joe, **163**

Scotch bonnet peppers, 49, 69, 119, 197. *See also* chile peppers

seafood: Chesapeake Corn and Crab Chowder, 60; Codfish Cakes, 87; Crab Stock, 199; Duck and Crawfish Gumbo, 62–63, **63**; Fried Croaker with Sweet Onion and Corn Hush Puppies, 92, 93; Frogmore Stew, **58**, 59; Maryland Crab Cakes, **80**, 81; NYC Oyster Pan Roast, Thomas Downing's, 79; Pickled Gulf Shrimp, **28**, 29; Salmon Croquettes, 90–91; Shrimp and Grits, 82–83, **83**; Whole Grilled Snapper with Creole Sauce, 86

Sea Island Red Peas, 46

Sea Salt–Spiced Cocktail Nuts, 140

Senegalese Peanut Soup, 71

sesame seeds. *See* benne seeds

shrimp: Frogmore Stew, **58**, 59; Pickled Gulf Shrimp, **28**, 29; Shrimp and Grits, 82–83, **83**

sides: Baked Macaroni and Cheese, 44, 45; Carolina Gold Rice Pilaf, 48; Corn Pudding, 39; Fried Green Tomatoes, 38; Fried Okra, **40**, 41; Ginger and Brown Sugar Candied Sweet Potatoes, 42; Hoppin' John, 46; Kale Sprouts with Sorghum and Benne, 33; Mixed Greens with Baby Turnips, **36**, 37; Red Beans and Rice, Louis Armstrong's, **50**, 51; Rice and Pigeon Peas, 49; Stewed Black-Eyed Peas, 35; Stewed Tomatoes and Okra, 30, **31**; Yankee Baked Beans, 43. *See also* salads

Siskind, Aaron, **160**

sit-ins, at lunch counters, **12**, 13, 76

Slow-Cooked Collards and Potlikker, 34

Smart-Grosvenor, Vertamae, 11, 18

"Smoking Hot" Oxtail Pepper Pot, 69

Smothered Turkey Grillades with Fried Apples, 94–95, **95**

snacks: Black-Eyed Pea Hummus, 142; Creole Spiced Boiled Peanuts, 141; Deviled Eggs, 137; Pimento Cheese, **138**, 139; Sea Salt–Spiced Cocktail Nuts, 140; Texas Caviar, 144, **145**

Snapper, Whole Grilled, with Creole Sauce, 86

SNCC (Student Nonviolent Coordinating Committee) sit-in, **12**

Son-of-a-Gun Stew, **66**, 67

sorghum: Kale Sprouts with Sorghum and Benne, 33; Spiced Sorghum Syrup, 105–06

soul food restaurants, 12, 103, 182

soups and stews, 52–71; Brunswick Stew, 68; Chesapeake Corn and Crab Chowder, 60; Collard, Tomato, and Cashew Stew, 61; Cowpea and Collard Soup, 65; Duck and Crawfish Gumbo, 62–63, **63**; Frogmore Stew, **58**, 59; gumbos, 18, 30, 32, 128; Okra and Tomato Soup, 64; Senegalese Peanut Soup, 71; "Smoking Hot" Oxtail Pepper Pot, 69; Son-of-a-Gun Stew, **66**, 67

Sparkling Watermelon and Lemon Verbena, 189

spice blends: Barbecue Dry Rub, 196; Creole Spice Blend, 196

Spiced Sorghum Syrup, 105–06

Spicy Pickled Okra, **130**, 134

stereotypes, 76, 132

Stewed Black-Eyed Peas, 35

Stewed Tomatoes and Okra, 30, **31**

stews. *See* soups and stews

Sticky Pork Ribs, 116–17, **117**

stocks, 199; Chicken Stock, 200; Crab
Stock, 199; Ham and Pork Stock, 200;
Veal Stock, 201; Vegetable Stock, 201

Stone-Ground Grits, 203. *See also* grits

stores and markets, 12, **55**, **160**, **163**

Student Nonviolent Coordinating
Committee (SNCC) sit-in, **12**

sugarcane cultivation, 177

Sweet Cherry Lemonade, **190**, 191

Sweet Home Café, **8–9**, 9, 13; list of
specials at, 204

Sweet Pea Tendril Salad, 22

sweet potatoes: Collard, Tomato, and
Cashew Stew, 61; Ginger and Brown
Sugar Candied Sweet Potatoes, 42;
Senegalese Peanut Soup, 71; Sweet
Potato Biscuits, **154**, 155; Sweet Potato
Pie, **166**, 167

sweets, 164–88; Banana Pudding, **184**, 185;
Basic Pie Crust, 164; Bourbon Pecan
Pie, **168**, 169; Buttermilk Tea Cakes,
176; Charleston Pecan Chewies, 181;
Chocolate Chess Pie, 165; Fried Apple
Hand Pies, 172–73, **173**; High Mesa
Peach and Blackberry Cobbler, **174**, 175;
Joe Froggers, 178, **179**; Lemon Curd
Blueberry Tart, 171; Lemon-Glazed
Pound Cake, 180; Lemon Meringue Pie,
170; Molasses Rum Raisin Cake, 177;
Peanut Brittle, 186, **187**; Pralines, 188;
Red Velvet Cake, 182–83, **183**; Sweet
Potato Pie, **166**, 167

Sweet Tea, Hibiscus and Ginger, 189

Sylvia's Restaurant, 12

syrups: Lemon Verbena, 189; Spiced
Sorghum, 105–06; Sweet Cherry,
190, 191

T

tarts: blind baking crust for, 164; Lemon
Curd Blueberry Tart, 171

Tea Cakes, Buttermilk, 176

teas, 18; Hibiscus and Ginger Sweet Tea,
189

Texas Caviar, 144, **145**

Thanksgiving foods: Ginger and Brown
Sugar Candied Sweet Potatoes, 42;
Sweet Potato Pie, **166**, 167

Toddle House sit-in, **12**

tomatoes: Baby Kale Salad with, **24**, 25;
Collard, Tomato, and Cashew Stew, 61;
Crab Stock with, 199; Creole Sauce,
Whole Grilled Snapper with, 86; Field
Green Salad with, 23; Fresh Tomato
Salsa, 122; Fried Green Tomatoes, 38;
Frogmore Stew, **58**, 59; green, Chow-
Chow with, **130**, 135; Ham and Tomato
Gravy, Chicken Livers and Grits with,
98, 99–100; Okra and Tomato Soup,
64; Roast Tomato Aioli, 38; Stewed
Tomatoes and Okra, 30, **31**; Texas
Caviar, 144, **145**; Tomato-Watermelon
Salad, 20, **21**

Tony the Peanut Man, 141

Trini Doubles, 121

Trout, Rainbow, Pan-Roasted, 88–89, **89**

Tulsa (OK), 56

Turkey Grillades, Smothered, with Fried
Apples, 94–95, **95**

turnips: Mixed Greens with Baby Turnips,
36, 37; Son-of-a-Gun Stew, **66**, 67

V

Veal Stock, 201

Vegetable Stock, 201

*Vibration Cooking, or the Travel Notes of a
Geechee Girl* (Smart-Grosvenor), 18

Vietnamese Spiced Chicken Wings, 96, **97**

The Virginia Housewife, or Methodical Cook
(Randolph), 32, 45

W

Waffles, Fried Chicken and, Hot, 105–06

walnuts: Sea Salt–Spiced Cocktail Nuts,
140

Washington, D.C., 12, **70**, **160**

Washington, George, 11, 76

watermelon, 132; Pickled Watermelon
Rind, **130**, 131; Sparkling Watermelon
and Lemon Verbena, 189; Tomato-
Watermelon Salad, 20, **21**

Wells (Harlem restaurant), 105

West African foods. *See* African foods
and influences

Western Range, 56–57; list of recipes
from, 206

West Indian foodways and recipes.
See Caribbean-influenced recipes

Wet Jerk Rub, 197

*What Mrs. Fisher Knows about Old Southern
Cooking: Soups, Pickles, Preserves, Etc.*
(Fisher), 56, 135

Williams, Milton, **70**, **75**

wiri wiri peppers, 69

Wright, Anthony, 141

Y

yams, 42

Yankee Baked Beans, 43

Yearwood, Lloyd W., **55**, **194**

Yellow Corn Bread, 151

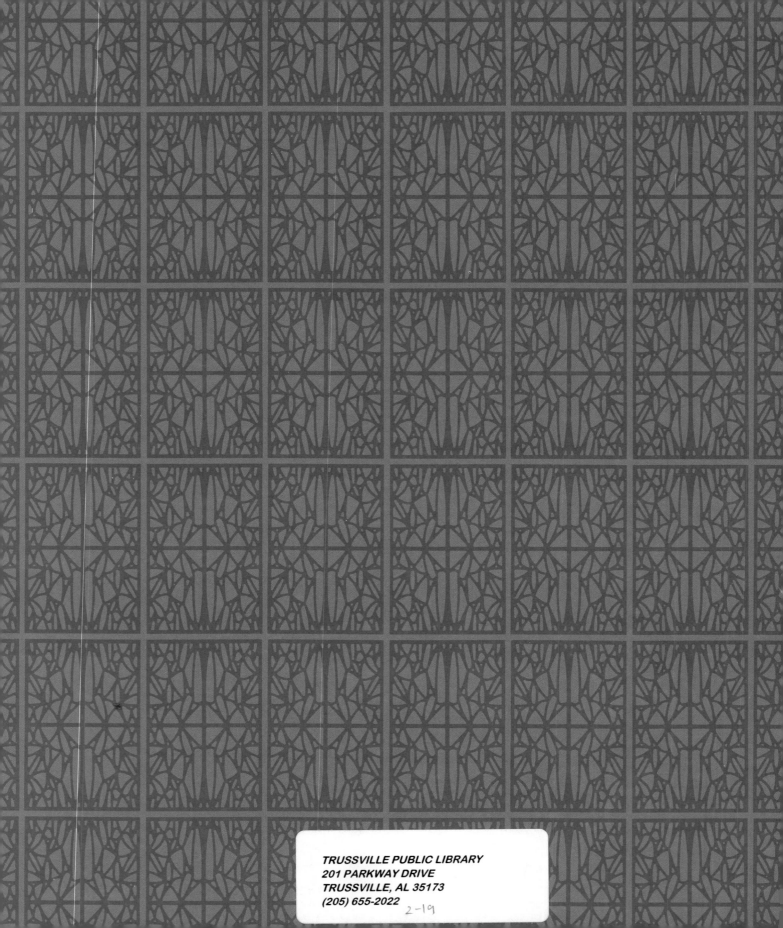